SECOND WORLD WAR LIVES

FAMILY HISTORY FROM PEN AND SWORD

Tracing Your Yorkshire Ancestors
Rachel Bellerby

•

The Great War Handbook
Geoff Brider

•

Tracing Your Royal Marine Ancestors
Richard Brooks and Matthew Little

•

Tracing Your Pauper Ancestors
Robert Burlison

•

Tracing Your East End Ancestors
Jane Cox

•

Tracing Your Labour Movement Ancestors
Mark Crail

•

Tracing Your Ancestors
Simon Fowler

•

Tracing Your Army Ancestors
Simon Fowler

•

A Guide to Military History on the Internet
Simon Fowler

•

Tracing Your Northern Ancestors
Keith Gregson

•

Your Irish Ancestors
Ian Maxwell

•

Tracing Your Northern Irish Ancestors
Ian Maxwell

•

Tracing Your Scottish Ancestors
Ian Maxwell

•

Tracing Your London Ancestors
Jonathan Oates

•

Tracing Family History on the Internet
Christopher Patton

•

Great War Lives
Paul Reed

•

Tracing Your Air Force Ancestors
Phil Tomaselli

•

Tracing Your Secret Service Ancestors
Phil Tomaselli

•

Tracing Your Criminal Ancestors
Stephen Wade

•

Tracing Your Legal Ancestors
Stephen Wade

•

Tracing Your Police Ancestors
Stephen Wade

•

Tracing Your Jewish Ancestors
Rosemary Wenzerul

•

Fishing and Fishermen
Martin Wilcox

•

How Our Ancestors Lived

SECOND WORLD WAR LIVES

A Guide for Family Historians

James Goulty

Published in association with the
Second World War Experience Centre
www.war-experience

Pen & Sword
FAMILY HISTORY

First published in Great Britain in 2012 by
PEN & SWORD FAMILY HISTORY
an imprint of
Pen & Sword Books Ltd
47 Church Street
Barnsley
South Yorkshire
S70 2AS

ISBN 978 1 84884 502 2

Typeset in Palatino and Optima by
Chic Media Ltd

Printed and bound in England by
CPI Group (UK) Ltd, Croydon, CR0 4YY

Pen & Sword Books Ltd incorporates the imprints of
Pen & Sword Aviation, Pen & Sword Family History, Pen & Sword Maritime,
Pen & Sword Military, Pen & Sword Discovery, Wharncliffe Local History,
Wharncliffe True Crime, Wharncliffe Transport, Pen & Sword Select,
Pen & Sword Military Classics, Leo Cooper, Remember When,
The Praetorian Press, Seaforth Publishing and Frontline Publishing

For a complete list of Pen & Sword titles please contact
PEN & SWORD BOOKS LTD
47 Church Street, Barnsley, South Yorkshire, S70 2AS, England
E-mail: enquiries@pen-and-sword.co.uk
Website: www.pen-and-sword.co.uk

CONTENTS

ACKNOWLEDGEMENTS

I wish to thank Rupert Harding, the commissioning editor of this title. It has been a great pleasure to work with him and benefit from his sound counsel, which has made the project that much more manageable. Equally, I am indebted to the Trustees of the Second World War Experience Centre for kind permission to use material from their archive, without which this book would have had to follow a different course.

As with any historical research project, there are a number of individuals who have lent support. I thank Cathy Pugh for initially inspiring me to tackle this book. I am especially grateful to Anne Wickes of the Second World War Experience Centre for all her assistance in dealing with my enquiries and to Jonathon, one of the Centre's volunteers, for scanning and copying photographs.

Stuart Eastwood, Curator of Cumbria's Military Museum (Border and King's Own Royal Border Regiment), was very helpful in providing material on Albert 'Ginger' Wilson. Paul Baillie, a highly experienced researcher particularly in the field of honours and awards, assisted in finding the DFC recommendation for Squadron Leader Denis Peto-Shepherd via his privately compiled index.

The Librarian at Royal Hospital Chelsea was extremely kind in allowing me to use their magnificent and valuable collection of regimental histories. While the staff at The National Archives, Kew provided every assistance. My thanks go to the Second World War Experience Centre, Cumbria's Military Museum, the Taylor Library and my brother Robert Goulty, who helped provide illustrations. Similarly, I am grateful to the North East Military Vehicle Club and the Shuttleworth Collection for allowing me to photograph vehicles and aircraft during their Annual DLI Rallies and Air Pageant 2010 respectively.

It has been a pleasure to correspond with surviving veterans and I am extremely grateful to Brian Aldiss; Ruth Aves; Sir Robin Dunn MC; Jean Gadsden; Bill Titchmarsh and Tony Tooth for agreeing to be included in the book. Last but not least, I thank my family and our dog Zephie for their unstinting love and support while researching and compiling this book.

ABBREVIATIONS

ATS	Auxiliary Territorial Service
BLG	Beach Landing Group
CFS	Central Flying School
CGS	Central Gunnery School
CO	Commanding Officer
FDS	Field Dressing Station
FOO	Forward Observation Officer
FTS	Flying Training School
HAA	Heavy Anti Aircraft
HAC	Honourable Artillery Company
ITW	Initial Training Wing
IWM	Imperial War Museum
LCP(L)	Landing Craft Personnel(Large)
LCT	Landing Craft Tank
LCVP	Landing Craft Vehicle Personnel
LDV	Local Defence Volunteers
LST	Landing Ship Tank
ML	Motor Launch
MOD	Ministry of Defence
MTB	Motor Torpedo Boat
NAAFI	Navy, Army and Air Force Institutes
NAM	National Army Museum
NCO	Non Commissioned Officer
OP	Observation Post
ORB	Operational Record Book
OTC	Officer Training Corps
OTU	Operational Training Unit
POW	Prisoner of War
RA	Royal Artillery
RAMC	Royal Army Medical Corps
RAOC	Royal Army Ordnance Corps
RCNR	Royal Canadian Naval Reserve
RHA	Royal Horse Artillery
RNVR	Royal Naval Volunteer Reserve
RSM	Regimental Sergeant Major

RW	Receiving Wing
SEAC	South East Asia Command
SFTS	Service Flying Training School
SWWEC	Second World War Experience Centre
TNA	The National Archives
UXB	Unexploded Bomb
WAAF	Women's Auxiliary Air Force
WOSB	War Office Selection Board
WRNS	Women's Royal Naval Service

INTRODUCTION

The Second World War remains the most destructive conflict in history. An estimated 50 million people lost their lives, at least twice as many as during the First World War. In reality this figure was likely to have been higher as it was difficult accurately to assess levels of casualties in wartime. Politically and militarily it has shaped the post-1945 world, acting as the catalyst for independence movements around the globe and leading to the Cold War, the ramifications of which we are still living with today. At the other extreme it continues to permeate our popular culture and language.

Arguably, during the war society bonded in a manner it has seldom done before or since, particularly during the dark days of 1940–1 when Britain stood alone against Nazi tyranny, and many cities endured heavy bombing. Survivors from the wartime generation are now in their eighties and nineties. In their youth they endured hardships scarcely imaginable to those of us from younger generations enjoying the relative comfort of our twenty-first-century lives. For them the war was a formative, frightening and fun experience. Many were given responsibilities at a young age that would have been unparalleled in peacetime and experienced close comradeship when under fire. One of the individuals featured in this book referred to the war as 'the biggest initiation rite in history'.

As the war progressed the armed services relied not only on regular personnel but also on volunteers and conscripts. These men and women came from a diverse range of social and educational backgrounds. All had to be trained to conduct a variety of tasks. This book traces the service of a handful of such individuals drawn mainly from the archives of the Second World War Experience Centre (SWWEC).

As a military historian it has been a privilege to delve into that archive to bring you their stories. Although thirteen individuals out of a war that affected millions may not appear very representative, I hope that the selection can be viewed as the war in microcosm from a British perspective.

Bert Blackmore and Colin Kitching take us to the war at sea. Both men initially served as ratings aboard surface vessels. The former was involved in the hunt for the *Bismarck*, while the latter took part in the capture of Enigma code tables from a German weather ship, the importance of which was not widely appreciated until after the war. They were subsequently commissioned. Bert volunteered for naval mine and bomb disposal work, seeing extensive service in Greece and finishing the war in the Far East. Colin went on to serve in a flotilla equipped with wooden 'Higgins boats' used for amphibious assaults, including Dieppe. Only later were these craft deployed on tasks better suited to their flimsy design, such as smoke laying.

The role of women in the armed forces is represented by two contrasting stories. Jean Gadsden joined the Women's Royal Naval Service (WRNS) or Wrens in 1943 and worked in signals distribution during D-Day before being involved in the decommissioning of coastal craft in 1945. Ruth Aves served in the Auxiliary Territorial Service (ATS) and saw action with Anti-Aircraft Command, particularly in the Bristol area. Both had to cope with the stress of wartime conditions and demonstrate that women could perform tasks as well as or even better than their male counterparts.

A professional soldier's experience is encapsulated by Sir Robin Dunn who after being commissioned into the Royal Artillery (RA) during the late 1930s served extensively in Europe and the Western Desert. He was awarded the Military Cross in Normandy while commanding a battery of self-propelled guns during June–July 1944.

Conversely, Bill Titchmarsh was a wartime conscript who was equally as determined to 'do his bit'. Having tired of being bullied by a non-commissioned officer (NCO) in Britain, he volunteered for an overseas posting as an infantryman, eventually seeing action in Italy including at Anzio, one of the bloodiest battles of the entire war.

Throughout the war the British made extensive use of 'special forces'. Albert Wilson fought with 1st Air Landing Brigade at Arnhem, having been flown in by glider to help secure drop zones for later parachute drops. While Eric de la Torre volunteered for the Commandos and was involved in the audacious raid on St Nazaire. Both men were captured by the Germans and so their war service encompasses prisoner of war experience too.

The war was not all about 'daring do' at the sharp end. Indeed, front-line troops would have been ineffective were it not for the efforts of support units. Dr Ian Campbell joined the Royal Army Medical Corps (RAMC) and treated casualties on D-Day and in subsequent operations. While Signalman Brian Aldiss slogged through the jungles of Burma and came under fire while helping to maintain adequate communications, a vital pre-requisite for the smooth running of 2nd Division.

Aerial combat is covered by two stories. Tony Tooth flew Spitfires on operations in the Mediterranean and shows us that popular conceptions about that aircraft's supposed prowess are not necessarily accurate. Later he went on to become a flying instructor in Rhodesia (now Zimbabwe), an experience that sparked a lifelong love affair with Africa.

Squadron Leader Denis Peto-Shepherd worked extensively in Flying Training Command, an overlooked area of the wartime RAF and one where several deaths occurred via accidents. Subsequently, he completed an operational tour over Europe flying Lancasters with No. 90 Squadron and was awarded the Distinguished Flying Cross.

A technical service like the RAF could never have operated without the efforts of ground crew and other support personnel. Albert Bennett became an instrument repairer, a trade that drew upon his civilian experience with office machines, and serviced aircraft in Britain and the Far East.

After each individual's story there is a research section explaining the sources used and highlighting materials you may wish to employ when considering your own wartime family history. Additionally, the book includes a general research guide dealing with major archives and resources that will hopefully set you off in the right direction.

James H. R. Goulty
January 2012

A GUIDE TO
SECOND WORLD WAR
RESEARCH

Before visiting an archive/museum it is helpful to try and ascertain what materials it holds that may assist with your research. Below is a general guide covering major archives/museums relevant when researching ordinary people caught up in the Second World War. Each chapter in this book is also followed by a research section. This outlines the specific materials used when dealing with that individual and provides pointers that might be helpful to the family historian interested in the wartime Armed Forces.

Additionally, it is always worth checking within your family whether a relative left any documents relating to their wartime experiences. Personal items such as letters, photographs and diaries along with any official documentation will all reveal clues about an individual's wartime service. Similarly, ask older members of your family for their recollections of the war, particularly so as to gain an impression of a relative's wartime experiences which may facilitate your research.

Service Records

Service Records and related documentation covering Second World War personnel are not available to the public, unlike for the First World War (although many of these records have been damaged). They are held by the Ministry of Defence (MOD) and only the veteran concerned or their next of kin are granted access. However, if you are a family member and have the consent of either of these parties you might be able to obtain copies of documents. Clearly, issues of privacy and data protection arise, especially if the individual concerned is still alive.

Service Records will not necessarily yield as much information as you think. Essentially, they were a record between employer and employee stating dates of service and where an individual served and with what unit/s. This will lead you onto other documentation such as War Diaries held by The National Archives (TNA). While Service Records don't state the operations an individual was involved in, they do provide details about their discharge; any reserve liability they incurred; medals awarded; and disciplinary record.

The first port of call should be: www.veterans-uk.info. The website contains up-to-date information on how to apply for a copy of a Service Record and any costs involved. It also provides contact details for the Army Personnel Centre and equivalent offices for the Navy and RAF. Be patient as it normally takes several months for requests to be processed.

Honours and Awards, c. 1939–45

Records of gallantry awards to wartime servicemen and women can be found at TNA. The Navy and Royal Marines are covered by ADM 12, ADM 1 and ADM 16. It helps to know when an award for gallantry was gazetted or appeared in the *London Gazette*, the official newspaper of state. This can be searched at: www.gazettes-online.co.uk, but the indexing can be awkward so you may still have to search for the original at TNA.

Surviving recommendations for awards for gallantry granted to soldiers (of all ranks) at TNA are in WO 373. Records for awards to RAF personnel are in AIR 2. As the chapter on Squadron Leader Peto-Shepherd explains, a privately held index has been created for this. For more information see, William Spencer, *Medals: The Researcher's Guide* (TNA, 2008).

During the Second World War eight campaign stars were granted for operational and non-operational service around the globe. The 1939–45 Star was awarded for active service between 3 September 1939 and 15 August 1945. The Atlantic Star was given for six months afloat in the Atlantic or Home Waters during the war. Some aircrew also qualified: the Air Crew Europe Star was awarded for at least two months operational flying from British bases over Europe including over Britain between 3 September 1939 and 4 June 1944. The Africa Star was awarded to men and women of the Armed Forces and Merchant Navy for involvement in North Africa between 10 June 1940 and 12 May 1943. It also encompassed service in Abyssinia, Somaliland, Eritrea and Malta. The Pacific Star and Burma Star were instituted for service in those theatres from December 1941 until August 1945. The Italy Star was for service during the Italian Campaign from 11 June 1943 until VE-Day (8 May 1945). The France and Germany Star was given for service in France, Belgium, Holland or Germany from D-Day until VE-Day.

All the stars were of a similar design but had different coloured ribbons symbolic of the theatre for which they were issued. They were manufactured from a yellow copper zinc alloy to form a six-pointed star with the Royal and Imperial cypher of King George VI at the centre surrounded by the name of the individual star. Unlike First World War campaign medals, those for the Second World War were not inscribed with the recipient's details.

Additionally, many service personnel were eligible for the Defence Medal and War Medal 1939–45. The former was awarded for three years' wartime service at home or six months' service abroad between 3 September 1939 and 2 September 1945 in a non-operational area subject to the threat of aerial attack. It was also conferred upon civilians who had been involved in Civil Defence and the Home Guard. The War Medal was granted to full-time personnel of the Armed Forces for twenty-eight days' service in both an operational and non-operational capacity. For further details see, Edward C. Joslin, *The Observer's Book of British Medals and Awards* (Frederick Warne & Co. Ltd, 1974) and H. Taprell Dorling, *Ribbons and Medals,* ed. and rev. A. Purves (Osprey, 1983).

Most records concerning wartime campaign medals are held by the MOD. However, information about the creation and various qualifications for the stars and medals exists at TNA. For the Army there is no equivalent to the First World War medal rolls but Service Records provide information on awards to individuals. For further information see, William Spencer, *Medals: The Researcher's Guide* (TNA, 2008).

Army, Navy and Air Force Lists

Army Lists continued to be produced during the Second World War. While they do not provide individual service histories, they can be used as a starting point for researching a wartime officer. They include details such as any honours or awards that an individual officer had received and the regiment/corps into which he was commissioned. For further information see, William Spencer, *Army Records: A Guide for Family Historians* (TNA, 2008). Similar lists exist for Navy and RAF officers and can be viewed at TNA, major museums and libraries.

Official Histories

There are numerous official histories covering the Second World War and those relevant to this book are listed below. Reference libraries may have copies of these and sets should be available at the museums and archives listed here. It is also worth looking out for any that might have been reprinted by Naval & Military Press.

Official histories will enhance your understanding of the war, particularly from a political and strategic standpoint, and help put an individual's personal experience into its wider context.

Ellis, L. F., *The War in France and Flanders, 1939–1940,* HMSO, 1953
_____, *Victory in the West, Vol. I, The Battle of Normandy,* HMSO, 1962
_____, *Victory in the West, Vol. II, The Defeat of Germany,* HMSO, 1968

Molony, C. J. C., *The Mediterranean and the Middle East, Vols V and VI*, HMSO, 1973 and 1984

Playfair, I. S. O., *The Mediterranean and the Middle East, Vols I, II, III and IV*, HMSO, 1945–66

Richards, D. and H. Saunders, *The Royal Air Force 1939–45, Vols I, II, III*, HMSO, 1953–4

Roskill, S. W., *The War at Sea Vols I, II, III and IV*, HMSO, 1954–61

Woodburn Kirby, S., *The War Against Japan Vols II, III, IV and V*, HMSO, 1958–69

Archives and Museums

The National Archives

Ruskin Avenue
Kew
Richmond
Surrey TW9 4DU
Tel: 020 8876 3444
Website: www.nationalarchives.gov.uk

A visit to TNA, Kew is a must for any family historian and will allow you to view a large range of official documents. To do so you need to obtain a reader's ticket and so bring the relevant forms of identification with you on your first visit. For more information on obtaining a reader's ticket and using TNA please see their website. TNA (formerly the Public Record Office) is the national archives of the British government and contains extensive holdings on the Second World War, including War Diaries and RAF Operational Record Books (ORB).

It is possible to view some documents online, but by no means all are available in a digital format, and in any case there is nothing like being able to research from original material for yourself. It helps if you can plan ahead and it is advisable to familiarise yourself with the TNA online catalogue, which gives a clear idea of the sort of material that is available. Remember once you have a reader's ticket you can order documents in advance which saves time. You should consult TNA guides, which can be downloaded from their website, and a selection of their 'guides for family historians' covering the Second World War are mentioned in the further reading section. Once there don't be afraid to ask staff for help, particularly as a large institution such as TNA can be daunting on an initial visit.

The Imperial War Museum

Lambeth Road
London SE1 6HZ
Tel: 020 7416 5320
Website: www.imw.org.uk

The reading room at the Imperial War Museum (IWM) is open to the public via appointment and there is an online catalogue which gives an indication of its holdings. Within the Department of Documents you will find numerous papers on the Second World War, including items such as personal letters, unpublished memoirs and training manuals/pamphlets. The Department of Books holds an extensive library of published materials, including contemporary journals and regimental histories. Additionally, the IWM house a Sound and Film Archive which incorporates a collection of oral history recordings covering the war plus a large selection of photographs and drawings. It is well worth checking whether the individual you wish to research was ever interviewed by the IWM. For more information please consult their website.

National War Museum of Scotland

Edinburgh Castle
Edinburgh EH1 2NG
Tel: 03001 236 789
Website: www.nms.ac.uk

This museum relates the military history of Scotland from *c.* 1600 to the present day and contains numerous exhibits, including a pristine 25-pounder field gun. There is a museum library that is open to the public on Tuesdays, 10 am–1 pm.

It has a wide selection of books, journals and other printed materials that may be consulted within the reading room.

National Army Museum

Royal Hospital Road
London SW3 4HT
Tel: 020 7730 0717
Website: www.national-army-museum.ac.uk

This houses one of the largest collections of military costume in the world and tells the history of the British Army from *c.* 1485 to the present day. A number of regimental collections, including those for the Middlesex Regiment and Women's Royal Army Corps, are maintained by the National Army Museum (NAM). The Templer Study Centre (TSC) has replaced the old reading room and houses an impressive collection of books and archives, including substantial Indian Army material. It is open to the public from Wednesday–Saturday, 10 am–5 pm and you must obtain a reader's ticket. Please consult their website for more information about applying for a reader's ticket and using the museum's facilities.

There is a diverse range of material on the Second World War, including a collection of training manuals/pamphlets which may shed light on the experience of ordinary soldiers. However, be warned, it can be difficult to access these as they don't always appear to be fully catalogued. NAM has a good collection of reference material such as the *Army Lists* and *London Gazette*.

A computerised catalogue can be consulted at the TSC together with NAM's old card index system. There is also a 'family history research guide' on their website.

National Maritime Museum

Greenwich
London SE10 9NF
Tel: 020 8858 4422
Website: www.mwm.ac.uk

The National Maritime Museum at Greenwich tells the story of Britain as a maritime nation with particular reference to the Merchant Navy and Royal Navy. The Caird Library incorporates standard works of reference such as the *Navy Lists* and houses numerous specialist books, collections of personal papers and photographs covering the Second World War. Before planning a visit it is worth consulting their online catalogue. The archives are especially helpful if you wish to research an individual merchant or Navy ship.

Royal Naval Museum

HM Naval Base (PP 66)
Portsmouth PO1 3NH
Tel: 023 9272 7562
Website: www.royalnavalmuseum.org

This museum houses an impressive archive and library, part of which originally belonged to the Admiralty. Its collections include approximately 22,000 photographic images, oral history recordings and materials relating to the WRNS. Be aware that the museum is on MOD property and you have to make an appointment and obtain a pass in order to visit. More details about this and the museum's collections can be found on their website.

RAF Museum

Graham Park Way
London NW9 5LL
Tel: 020 8205 2266
Website: www.rafmuseum.org.uk

The RAF Museum, situated at the former London Aerodrome, Hendon, houses an impressive library and archive. These facilities are open to the public via appointment only and you need to make the nature of your research interests clear. For more information about using the reading room and gaining access to the collections please visit their website.

In particular they hold a large collection of log books and personal papers that span the world wars. These range from material relating to important figures such as 'Bomber' Harris to items dealing with ordinary airmen. There are extensive holdings of books and maps on most aspects of aviation within the library. Their archives enable you to trace the history of individual aircraft via sources such as Aircraft Movement Cards (Form 78) and Aircraft Crash Cards.

Fleet Air Arm Museum

RNAS Yeovilton
Ilchester BA22 8HT
Tel: 01935 840 565
Website: www.fleetairarm.com

Research is by appointment as their reading room has limited capacity and is only open Wednesdays–Fridays. The museum houses an extensive photographic collection and a variety of archival sources. These include personal papers on leading figures in the history of naval aviation; Squadron Line Books (equivalent to ORBs); records on individual aircraft; and those for ratings from the Royal Naval Reserve, *c.* 1908–55.

Royal Marines Museum

Eastney Barracks
Southsea PO4 9PX
Tel: 01705 819 385
Website: www.royalmarinesmuseum.co.uk

The museum traces the history of the Royal Marines from *c.* 1664 to the present day and houses an impressive library incorporating around 1 million documents, a substantial photographic collection and historic artefacts.

The Second World War Experience Centre

1A Rudgate Court
Walton near Wetherby
West Yorkshire LS23 7BF
Tel: 01937 541 274
Website: www.war-experience.org

The SWWEC's mission is to collect, preserve and encourage access to the surviving testimony of men and women who lived through the Second World War in whatever capacity and of whatever age. Consequently, the centre's archive comprises a diverse range of material and more information exists for some individuals than others. In addition to personnel from the Armed Forces, it covers civilians on the Home Front, school children, foreign nationals throughout Europe, the Commonwealth and the USA, and British civilians living overseas.

The archive includes written accounts and recollections, as well as contemporary wartime documents, photographs, diaries, scrapbooks, maps and memorabilia. Additionally, it holds over 4,000 recordings of interviews with people talking about their wartime experiences, many of which have been transcribed. Transcript copies and copies of the original recordings are available on request. It is well worth checking whether the individual you are interested in has been recorded by the centre, or has donated material.

The centre produces a bi-annual journal, *Everyone's War*, which is themed on a particular aspect of the war, such as a specific campaign or item of weaponry, that relies extensively on material from their archive. Members of the centre's friends association receive a copy of each journal on publication and back issues are available to purchase by anyone on request.

Visitors are welcome at the centre by prior appointment. Their website contains further information and useful links that may help with your research. No online catalogue exists but their website provides a flavour of the type of material held by the centre. Hard copies of their catalogue can be consulted within the reading room when you visit.

Liddle Collection

Special Collections
The Brotherton Library
University of Leeds
Leeds LS2 9JT
Tel: 01133 435 518
Website: www.leeds.ac.uk/library/spcoll/liddle

The Liddle Collection was founded over thirty years ago to preserve evidence relevant to first-hand experiences of the First World War. Additionally, it has a selection of personal papers and other material relating to the Second World War and a catalogue of its holdings can be found online.

Regimental/Corps Museums

In Britain there is a rich diversity of regimental/corps museums that not only tell the history of local units, but also reflect the wider heritage of the Army and the country as a whole. To a lesser or greater extent all cover the Second World War. Some, like the Durham Light Infantry, have entrusted their archives to local record offices, while others remain attached to museums and are overseen by a small, dedicated staff who are often former members of the regiment concerned.

While they may not necessarily have significant material on the individual soldier you wish to research, they will hold related items. This includes material such as regimental journals and histories, enlistment registers, POW lists, War Diaries and possibly correspondence with veterans. There is often more information to be found on officers than that available for other ranks.

To find your nearest regimental museum, or the one most relevant to your research, see: www.armymuseums.org.uk, which will direct you to the Army Museums Ogilby Trust. If you wish to make a research enquiry it is best done via a letter and it will be appreciated if you include an SAE. Another useful source of information on regimental museums is Terence and Shirley Wise's

A Guide to Military Museums & Other Places of Interest 10th Revised Edition (Terence Wise, 2001), but be warned that the details of some museums may have changed since this was published.

Commonwealth War Graves Commission

If you are interested in a serviceman or woman who was killed during the war, then this is the place to start your search. The commission's website lists details of at least 1.7 million individuals known to have been killed during the world wars and provides information on where they are buried or commemorated. This includes civilians killed during the Second World War. For more information see: www.cwgc.org.

Society of Genealogists

14 Charterhouse Buildings
Goswell Road
London EC1M 7BA
Tel: 020 7251 8199
Website: www.sog.org.uk

The society's library has material on the Second World War, including the *Army Lists* and *Navy Lists*, numerous regimental histories and other books which can be searched for via their online catalogue. They provide a range of CD-ROMs and maintain an extensive website which you are advised to consult, particularly for up-to-date information on the cost of using their facilities and details such as opening hours.

Chapter 1

An Artillery Officer in Europe and North Africa – the Right Honourable Sir Robin Dunn MC

As he grew up there was little doubt that Robin Dunn would become a soldier. His father and both grandfathers were Army officers and one of his great-grandfathers had served with the Horse Artillery in the Peninsular War, eventually becoming a major general. He was born in Trowbridge in January 1918 and his first memories consisted of 'trumpet calls, reveille, officer's mess, last post, the shouts of words of command, the stamping of feet and the smell of ammonia in the troop stables'.[1]

Robin was educated at St Aubyns, a preparatory school in Rottingdean, before going onto Wellington College just as Hitler was coming to power. While there he developed an aptitude for running and led the long-distance running team. By his own admission he claimed not to have shone academically or been particularly talented at other games. However, for three seasons he captained 'the Occasionals', a cricket team consisting of staff and senior boys that played local village sides and regiments from Aldershot.

In 1936 Robin attended the Royal Military Academy at Woolwich. Known as 'the Shop', an abbreviation of workshop, it was founded in 1741 to train officer cadets for artillery and later engineer regiments. His father had been Adjutant at Woolwich so he knew what standards were expected of cadets. He recalled that it provided, 'a very high class education and you were encouraged to work. The discipline was even stricter than Sandhurst . . . I have never been so fit in my life, . . . We used to do physical training and infantry drill every day constantly in the gymnasium.'[2]

Even though the RA was in the process of mechanization, horse riding featured heavily on the syllabus. Robin spent much time riding, was second in the Saddle, the Royal Military Academy riding prize, and participated in drag hunts organised by the RA in Kent and Essex. At the end of the eighteen-month course he was awarded the Sword of Honour, given to the best performing cadet, and several other prizes.

Subsequently, he attended a Young Officers' course at the School of Artillery, Larkhill. This was extremely beneficial as it was professionally tailored on the ranges so that officers practised the role of every member of a field battery from the battery commander down to the ammunition number on an individual gun. Afterwards he undertook a driving and maintenance course at Woolwich before being posted to 7th Field Regiment RA in late summer 1938.

The 7th Field was part of 3rd Division and destined to serve with the British Expeditionary Force (BEF) in France and Belgium during 1939–40. When Robin joined them the guns were being withdrawn so they could be re-bored from 18-pounder into 25-pounder weapons and the regiment was operating at a highly reduced establishment. However, it was brought up to strength with reservists and by October 1939 had deployed to France.

Fortunately, the conditions of the 'Phoney War' ensured that 7th Field could instigate instruction on gunnery matters that made up for its lack of collective training in Britain. They were stationed near Lille and Robin learnt to speak French from the locals and as a result picked up a Lillois accent.

Initially, 7th Field was involved in fortifying the Belgian frontier. Additionally, Major General (later Field Marshal) Montgomery, the divisional commander, instituted a series of exercises that kept the troops on their toes. These entailed units of the BEF advancing beyond their fixed defences and mounting a series of defensive engagements before launching a counter-attack. This proved very similar to what was required when the Germans actually invaded Belgium on 10 May 1940.

Robin cut his teeth under fire as an OP (Observation Post) officer, mainly supporting a battalion from the Grenadier Guards. He discovered that enemy shelling was particularly unpleasant owing to its accuracy, whereas the regular bombing and strafing attacks endured by British troops appeared to cause fewer casualties, even when the Luftwaffe employed the dreaded Stuka dive-bomber.

Although a junior officer, he commanded a troop of guns overlooking Louvain, 'I remember seeing all the bridges along the river go up and the Belgian Army, most of whom were horse drawn . . . came back over the river and we knew even then we were face to face with the Germans, and the Germans attacked and there was some very fierce fighting . . .'.[3]

By 16 May the Germans had burst through on the right of 1st Division and consequently 7th Field was pulled back to the River Dendre on the other side of Brussels. Robin's troop worked under the divisional rearguard and each gun had around 600 rounds dumped with it. He recalled 'the guns were red hot . . . the gunners were working like slaves, stripped to the waist'.[4] They could not understand it when ordered to retreat but the Germans had breached the French lines near Sedan and now the British ran the risk of being cut off.

The regiment would eventually form part of the perimeter at Dunkirk. Despite the confused nature of the fighting throughout May 1940, 7th Field occupied some formidable positions, particularly near Thumesnil. Here the 25-pounder field guns were dispersed around a farm that was heavily fortified with local materials and blessed with natural camouflage. This included a road to its front that hid track and blast marks. As he stated, 'nothing but a direct hit on each gun pit [which were carefully hidden] would have knocked us out'.[5]

By late May the overall situation had worsened considerably with the Belgians buckling under German pressure and the French unable to counter-attack successfully. Robin attended a conference held by his glum-faced Commanding Officer (CO). The BEF's position had become unsustainable and an evacuation was to be organised.

> We removed all the optical instruments and everything from the guns. Disabled them as far as we could, and we were in action at La Panne along the sand dunes along the edge of the beach, and we marched down onto the beach and we waded out up to our armpits in water. I had my best uniform on. A very expensive tunic, which I bought from a well known tailor.[6]

Back in Britain, Robin was amazed to find that after their humiliation at Dunkirk British troops were nevertheless greeted as heroes. The 3rd Division concentrated in Somerset and was rapidly re-equipped ahead of a planned deployment across the Channel but then the French surrendered. Robin discovered that he had been recommended for the Military Cross for his conduct in France but this was downgraded to a Mention in Dispatches.

Wartime acting ranks were introduced so as a troop commander he was promoted from second lieutenant straight to captain. His regiment adjusted to their new role as an anti-invasion force, in case the Germans landed, and undertook exercises in the Cotswolds. During the winter of 1940–1 he served as a gunnery instructor at 3rd Division's battle school. He was then posted to

11th Honourable Artillery Company (HAC) Royal Horse Artillery (RHA), a proud and prestigious Territorial regiment based in Surrey.

The HAC had performed badly during training at Larkhill and to remedy the situation regular officers were being drafted in. By the summer of 1941 they were earmarked for deployment to the Middle East in support of 1st Armoured Division. In October, a month to the day after he had married, Robin sailed aboard the 'SS *Samaria*, an old Cunarder built for the North Atlantic run'.[7] The voyage to Suez was a lengthy experience via the Cape. The officers were able to travel in comparative luxury but other ranks had to endure the overcrowded, sweaty and vomit-ridden conditions of the troop decks.

The HAC were still equipped with towed 25-pounder field guns that despite their high silhouette were a formidable weapon. As one historian and former wartime gunner explained:

> Taking 11,000 yards as the fighting range of a 25-pounder, and putting it 3,000 yards behind the forward troops and allowing it an arc of 90° some rough arithmetic showed a single gun could have a possible target area of 30 square miles. A regiment of twenty-four 25-pounders, firing at three rounds per gun per minute [normal rate] could place rather more than three quarters of a ton of steel and high explosive on a target . . .[8]

The Western Desert with its expanses of open country uncluttered by civilian populations appeared to offer a tactician's paradise, especially for exponents of armoured warfare. However, the British consistently failed to engender the necessary combined arms co-operation and would initially often commit units piecemeal with dire consequences.

Robin experienced the desert largely as an OP officer in an American-built M3 Stuart light tank known as the 'Honey' by British forces. This would enable him to keep pace with armoured units and direct the guns in battle as required. He remembered that he 'enjoyed the technique of a FOO [Forward Observation Officer], finding my way alone across the desert to a suitable OP, watching the fall of shot and correcting the fire onto the target . . . the easy companionship of my tank crew and the feeling of relaxation when at night we moved into close leaguer'.[9]

Recalling his first desert action near El Agheila, Libya he noted:

> we bore the brunt of that attack. There were some very bad sand dunes where we were and the German tanks appeared one morning. I was at my OP and suddenly we saw these tanks moving up towards us and

we started to retreat but a lot of the guns got stuck in the sand dunes, and eventually we were caught in the middle of the desert by a column of about thirty or forty tanks, and we knocked out quite a lot of them. I was standing just behind the gun line and I was hit in the side and I thought it was just a glancing blow.[10]

Nearly sixty years later an X-ray revealed that he still had a fragment of shrapnel in his lung from this encounter back in early 1942.

Knightsbridge was the name given to a key tactical feature or box that formed part of the Gazala Line. In late May 1942 the line was attacked by Rommel's Afrika Korps with Italian support in what became an epic fifty-two-day struggle during which the HAC suffered its worst casualties of the entire war. By the end of the Battle of Gazala its total casualties 'were 37 officers and 475 ORs [other ranks]' and according to one account it was 'impossible to describe the fighting, the endurance, the humour and the tragedy which these figures represent'.[11]

Eventually, the British retreated which precipitated the fall of Tobruk and left 8th Army within 60 miles of Alexandria. Partly this was caused by deficiencies in the Gazala Line. Too few infantry units were based in the south and many of the defences, notably at Tobruk, were in disrepair. The tying up of significant numbers of troops in defensive boxes also proved a hindrance rather than an asset.

At Knightsbridge Robin continued his work as an OP officer, roaming the battlefield in his light tank in order to observe and direct fire. On 14 June he was sent out through a minefield as the remnants of 1st Armoured Division, including the HAC, were tasked with covering a gap between the Eluet-El-Tamar and Acroma Boxes, which continued to resist the enemy.

Robin and his crew were thwarted by a sandstorm and sat this out. Then on climbing back into his tank Robin was struck by a bullet that passed through his hat sending blood pouring down his face. He received permission to have his wound dressed and on returning through the minefield was surprised to be confronted by fifteen German tanks.

I felt rather like a rabbit, you know, bolted out of a cover. I turned down the minefield and I could see the tracer and eventually there was a crash in the side of the tank and the tank stopped, and so I said to the driver 'Go on Finneron,' and to my astonishment the tank drove on ... although they had drilled a hole in the tank they hadn't actually hit the track ... then I looked down. There was a scene of absolute chaos inside the turret. The wireless operator and the gunner were obviously badly

Troops and equipment being unloaded at Queen Beach during D-Day. Note the Sherman Crab flail tank for use in clearing minefields, one of the many 'funnies' employed by British forces. (Taylor Library)

wounded, and then I looked down at my own leg and there was a huge hole in my knee . . .[12]

After a nightmarish journey Robin was evacuated to the former Italian hospital at Tobruk. Here his wound was treated and encased in a 'Tobruk plaster', a special form of splint designed for use under desert conditions.[13] By now Tobruk was in danger of being overwhelmed by the enemy and Robin was among the last casualties who were able to leave aboard an ambulance crewed by American Quakers. They managed to ferry him to Mersa Metruh where he spent some time in hospital prior to being evacuated to South Africa. As 8th Army was being thrown back towards Alexandria in turmoil it had been decided to evacuate casualties to hospitals out of theatre if possible.

In South Africa Robin recuperated at a large military hospital in Pietermaritzburg, where he was welcomed by the sight of many beautiful young nurses. However, he was keen to be posted back to Britain, especially as his wife had given birth to their first child. In September 1942 a medical board granted him passage to Britain as they felt he should enjoy the rest of his convalescence at home. He boarded a Union Castle boat taking wounded home plus a large cargo of oranges destined for British infants.

On returning he was promoted major and given command of 16th Field Battery in his old regiment. They were still part of 3rd Division and as they were to be in the vanguard on D-Day were being re-equipped with the American-built 105mm Howitzer Motor Carriage. This was a self-propelled gun christened 'Priest' by the British owing to its anti-aircraft machine gun in a 'pulpit'-like mounting.

These tank-like vehicles necessitated a degree of retraining, especially for drivers. Gunners had to familiarise themselves with new fire control mechanisms and 105mm ammunition that was not standard issue in the British Army. Additionally, vehicles had to be waterproofed and personnel practised in co-operation with other units ahead of D-Day.

Throughout 1943 and early 1944 Robin was engaged in intensive training with 7th Field, initially in Scotland and later Sussex with the rest of 3rd Division. On 1 June 1944 his CO Colonel (later Major General Sir Nigel) Tapp DSO noted, 'The Regiment is now fully equipped and has carried out three or four rehearsals for invasion and is now awaiting with some impatience the signal to start. It is four years to the day that the Regiment, some thirty to forty per cent of whom are still present, left the beaches at Dunkirk.'[14]

The unit loaded into landing craft at Portsmouth on 4 June, but was delayed for 24 hours owing to bad weather. They sat waiting in their Landing Craft Tanks (LCTs) watching the WRNS boat crews in the harbour, which provided a welcome distraction for the soldiers. On D-Day 7th Field was required to mount a 'run-in shoot' firing from their landing craft at Queen Beach, a sector of Sword Beach and something for which they had practised in Scotland. The Priests were loaded four to a LCT 'in pairs so that there were 18 LCTs carrying the 72 guns of the 3 regiments of the 3rd Division Artillery and the LCTs sailed in arrowhead formation with 7th Field leading'.[15] A motor launch with radar helped calculate the range and FOOs from each regiment observed the fire from smaller craft.

It was an amazing sight to witness dozens of landing craft with the bombarding squadron Royal Navy led by HMS *Warspite* on their left flank. The Priests opened fire at maximum range and gradually dropped the range as they approached the beach. This neutralising fire was so effective, as one FOO noted, that it almost all fell within an area dominated by a German strongpoint. For the enemy this must have been demoralising, particularly when they saw the scale of the oncoming invasion fleet. At H-hour Robin had a grandstand view from the bridge of his LCT, 'these amphibious tanks landing and then the assault infantry in their landing craft running up the beach and these various . . ."funnies"'.[16] These were specialist armoured vehicles intended to clear beach obstacles and tackle fortifications.

7th Field landed at 10.45am, or H+195 minutes, and it was Robin's task to ensure all twenty-four guns of the regiment exited the beach as quickly as possible so that they could take up positions at Hermanville. This was not straightforward as the beach was littered with burnt-out tanks and crowded with troops and vehicles from various units desperate to make progress. Moreover, the Staffordshire Yeomanry had halted not far inland causing a traffic jam as they removed waterproofing from their tanks and brewed up.

Eventually, the guns came into action '800 yards up the road towards Colleville, at the exact spot on which we had decided from aeroplane photographs during briefing'.[17] Subsequently, Robin was intimately involved in providing artillery support for 1st Battalion Royal Norfolk Regiment. They were to assault a strongpoint code-named Hillman on the Perrier Ridge before pushing onto a forward assembly area designated Rover.

Ideally, the 15in guns of HMS *Warspite* would have been employed against Hillman but communications with the ship had broken down. Consequently, Robin advanced on foot with the infantry and attempted to give effective support. As the operation progressed it became clear that the Norfolks might be able to bypass the enemy. Robin noted:

> We had about a mile and a half to go to Rover, which was a wooded area on the top of a gentle rise, with the ground falling away more sharply beyond. Our way lay across a single very large cornfield, with standing corn. Most of the way was traversed on our hands and knees, and by what I believe the infantry call 'rushes'. The whole area was covered by the machine guns of Hillman.[18]

From the Norfolks two companies became pinned down by Hillman, having advanced too close to it, while the remainder had a tough job clearing the woods. Even so, by 7pm Rover was occupied. Robin stayed with the infantry to provide fire support but this proved unnecessary as the enemy never counter-attacked.

Overall the D-Day landings had been a success but the Allies now became embroiled in a battle of attrition in Normandy. In front of Caen the British and Canadians experienced some of the bitterest fighting of the campaign. During 7–8 July Operation Charnwood was launched to seize Caen. It was preceded by a raid by 450 Halifax and Lancaster bombers. These blasted the ancient city with 2,500 tons of bombs, much to the amazement of many British troops including Robin.

> We attacked at a quarter past four in the morning, and I was with the battalion commander of 1st Norfolks, which was the battalion I had supported on D-Day, and I had a portable wireless set back to the guns and we walked up from the start line just behind the assaulting companies. The noise was deafening, you couldn't hear yourself think. There were about three divisional artilleries firing on our front and the objective was a place called Lebisey Wood.[19]

The troops dug in at Lebisey Wood and soon came under fire from a German battery on the other side of the River Orne. Robin recalled:

> I was hit in the head and I fell down and couldn't speak, but I could think. In fact I wrote out a fire order and gave it to my signaller, and then a couple of stretcher bearers arrived, and we were still under heavy shell fire . . . and I went back to the RAP [Regimental Aid Post] and then a casualty clearing station, by which time I had been given . . . another stiff shot of morphia and was put aboard a LST [Landing Ship Tank] . . . to evacuate stretcher cases, and I got back to England.[20]

Throughout the action Robin had tirelessly supported the infantry and kept his communications with the guns in tact even when wounded. He was eventually awarded the Military Cross for his actions. His citation noted that he refused treatment until ordered to by CO 1st Norfolks and 'under heavy fire exhibited a calm and resolute bearing which was an example both to his own party and the infantry'.[21]

Returning to Britain, Robin had the shell splinter removed from his skull and ended up in a civilian hospital in Stratford-upon-Avon, where he was misdiagnosed with shell shock. Fortunately, a relative who worked for the Red Cross discovered him. He was able to receive some specialist treatment and speech therapy under Professor Hugh Cairns at St Hugh's College, Oxford. By October 1944 he was back commanding 16th Battery 7th Field near Venlo on the River Maas, Holland. While he was sad to leave his family in Britain, as his second child had now been born, he was relieved to be with his old regiment rather than to have been posted elsewhere.

Soon after he arrived 16th Battery was supporting armoured cars from the Household Cavalry and spent most of the winter of 1944–5 'sniping away' at the Germans. Conditions were wet and cold and frequently ammunition was rationed, particularly for routine tasks. On one occasion Robin decided to save

Major R. W. D. Dunn (RA) being awarded the Military Cross by Field Marshal Montgomery in Holland, November 1944. (SWWEC)

up a week's ration and hit the enemy when they had grown careless and exposed themselves on their positions, having become accustomed to the absence of British artillery. The resulting 'stonk' was successful and accurate.

During the spring of 1945 7th Field was deployed to the Reichswald as the British attempted to 'turn' the defences of the Siegfried Line. They faced fanatical young German troops from First Parachute Army desperate to defend the Fatherland and endured appalling muddy conditions in awkward terrain that negated the effectiveness of armour.

During the battle Robin experienced something that disturbed him even more than both of his wounds.

I was leading this column along a track and a whole lot of German soldiers came running out shouting 'minen, minen' and so I stopped and said . . . 'Do you know a way through the minefield?' and they said 'ja, ja.' So I put one of the German soldiers into the carrier [Universal Carrier, a small tracked box-like armoured vehicle] in front of my carrier and on we went, and I was the second carrier in the column, and I said 'He is to lead the way through the mines.' And we hadn't gone very far when there was a bang and a puff of smoke and this wretched German soldier was thrown out of the top of the carrier and landed dead on the ground. So I got out of my carrier and I walked up and had a look at him. When I came back my driver said 'Just look behind the carrier Sir.'. . . . you could see the shiny top of the mine with nothing on it and we hadn't set it off . . . a most unpleasant experience and it really shook me . . .[22]

Shortly after the battle an unexpected piece of news arrived. Robin was to be posted to command 'C' Battery 4th RHA. Although he felt it was a shame to leave the battery he had trained and commanded in battle, it was pleasing to be given command of a unit in the elite RHA. As he joined them 4th RHA was readying itself to cross the Rhine but a bout of influenza deprived him of seeing action with his new battery until they reached Wesel.

Throughout the closing stages of the war in Europe Robin's unit supported 4th Armoured Brigade, an independent brigade comprising a motor battalion and three armoured regiments besides 4th RHA and commanded by 35-year-old Mike (later field Marshal Lord) Carver. They were involved in a serious battle near Verden on the River Aller but otherwise experienced no major combat before entering war-ravaged Hamburg on VE-Day.

Robin remained in the Army but quickly discovered that peacetime postings lacked the dynamism of wartime service. After a period at staff

The 'Jeep' was a familiar sight to Allied soldiers in North-West Europe c. 1944–5 and was used for a variety of tasks. This restored Willys MB is resplendent in the markings of 3rd Division, to which Robin belonged. (Author's photograph)

college, he was posted to India which ensured yet more separation from his young family. He decided to read for the Bar and eventually left the Army in 1948. During the war he had encountered many fearful situations and witnessed the camaraderie of soldiers under fire. While he was keen to put his Army service behind him, the experience it provided proved highly beneficial in his future career as a barrister and judge.

Researching the Right Honourable Sir Robin Dunn

Robin Dunn's _Sword and Wig: Memoirs of a Lord Justice_ (Quiller Press, 1993) provides more detail on his Army service, including his criticisms of the High Command in the Western Desert prior to Montgomery assuming command, and of his divisional and brigade commanders on D-Day. Another particularly interesting feature of his memoirs is the inclusion of his wartime diaries covering France 1940 and Knightsbridge 1942. Additionally, Sir Robin was interviewed by Dr Peter Liddle on behalf of SWWEC in July 2002. This recorded useful information particularly on the Western Desert and Normandy and a transcript is available at their archives. A further interview with Sir Robin Dunn MC entitled 'Gunners on D-Day (6 June 1944)' was conducted by Major H. S. T. Spender (RA) in 1994 to mark the fiftieth anniversary of D-Day. A copy of the transcript is available at SWWEC and the RA archives at Woolwich.

A search of the National Register of Archives revealed that Sir Robin deposited material relating to his service _c._ 1940–2 at the IWM (Department of Documents), London. The National Register of Archives can be consulted via TNA website and is useful when trying to establish the existence of any personal papers that may assist research on an individual.

War Diaries for 7th Field and 4th RHA spanning Sir Robin's service can be found at TNA within WO 167 BEF France and WO 171 Allied Expeditionary Force N.W. Europe. These provided useful information on training and operational experience, particularly with regard to Normandy, including a report on D-Day that Sir Robin was asked to write as battery commander. Even if you are not researching an officer, War Diaries will still prove useful in detailing the movements and activities of units. Similarly, when researching a specific incident relating to a gunner a useful tip is to consider who they were supporting and consult the relevant War Diaries for those units too.

WO 204 Allied Forces, Mediterranean, Military HQ Papers contains an interesting narrative on the wartime service of the HAC that was compiled in

1945 with considerable assistance from Captain Peter Thompson-Glover, the Adjutant and his staff. WO 373 War Office and MOD Military Secretary's Department: Recommendations Honours and Awards for Gallantry and Distinguished Service (Army) contains the recommendation for Sir Robin's MC. Details of awards can be searched online via TNA website, but his actual recommendation was viewed on microfilm which requires patience to trawl through.

The archives of the Firepower Royal Artillery Museum at Woolwich also hold War Diaries for artillery units, as well as an extensive collection of wartime pamphlets/training manuals and other materials. Be warned, they levy a charge for private research and for up-to-date information see: www.firepower.org.uk. Similarly, the HAC has its own museum and archives in London and for further information see: www.hac.org.uk.

Shelford Bidwell's *Gunners at War: A Tactical Study of the Royal Artillery in the Twentieth Century* (Arms & Armour Press, 1970) is a tactical study of the RA with a strong emphasis on the experience of the world wars. Similarly, Ian V. Hogg's *British & American Artillery of World War Two* (Arms and Armour Press, 1978) is an invaluable reference tool detailing all the main types of guns deployed and their capabilities.

Major General Julian Thompson's *Dunkirk Retreat To Victory* (Pan Books, 2009) draws upon a wide range of material, including Sir Robin's reminiscences, to offer a detailed account of the situation that befell the BEF during May–June 1940. David. G. Chandler's 'The Fight at Gazala Western Desert February/June 1942', in *Purnell's History of the Second World War* (Phoebus Publishing Ltd, 1967), Vol. 3, No. 5, is a thought-provoking read. While the late Field Marshal Lord Carver's *Dilemmas of the Desert War* (Spellmount Ltd, 2002) is a classic work covering the Libyan Campaign 1940–2.

Eversley Belfield and H. Essame's *The Battle for Normandy* (Pan Books, 1983), Max Hastings's *Overlord D-Day and the Battle for Normandy 1944* (Papermac, 1993) and Carlo D'Este's *Decision in Normandy* (Robson Books, 2000) provide stimulating perspectives on the Normandy campaign, including the British experience at Sword Beach. John North's *North-West Europe 1944–45: The Achievement of 21st Army Group* (HMSO, 1953) is a very readable semi-official history outlining the advance from Normandy to Germany.

Notes

1. Robin Dunn, *Sword and Wig: Memoirs of a Lord Justice* (Quiller Press, 1993), p. 1.
2. Second World War Experience Centre, Acc. No. 2001-1141, transcript of interview by Dr Peter Liddle with the Right Honourable Sir Robin Dunn, tape 1500, July 2002, p. 2.
3. Ibid., p. 4.
4. Dunn, *Sword and Wig*, p. 257.
5. Ibid., p. 261.
6. SWWEC, Acc. No. 2001-1141, transcript of interview by Dr Peter Liddle with the Right Honourable Sir Robin Dunn, tape 1500, July 2002, p. 5.
7. Dunn, *Sword and Wig*, p. 29.
8. Shelford Bidwell, *Gunners at War: A Tactical Study of the Royal Artillery in the Twentieth Century* (Arms & Armour Press, 1970), p. 139.
9. Dunn, *Sword and Wig*, p. 46.
10. SWWEC, Acc. No. 2001-1141, transcript of interview by Dr Peter Liddle with the Right Honourable Sir Robin Dunn, tape 1500, July 2002, p. 7.
11. The National Archives, WO 204/8329, 11 HAC RHA History 1939–45, p. 38.
12. SWWEC, Acc. No. 2001-1141, transcript of interview by Dr Peter Liddle with the Right Honourable Sir Robin Dunn, tape 1500, July 2002, p. 8.
13. For more details on the 'Tobruk plaster', see Redmond McLaughlin, *The Royal Army Medical Corps* (Leo Cooper, 1972), pp. 66–7.
14. TNA, WO 171/969, War Diary 7th Field Regiment RA June 1944, Summary of Major Events – Jan to May 1944, paragraph 6 Conclusion signed by CO 7th Field Regiment RA.
15. Transcript of interview with Sir Robin Dunn MC, 'Gunners on D-Day (6 June 1944)' by Major H. S. T. Spender RA, 29 March 1994 (as part of the fiftieth anniversary of D-Day), p. 1. (A copy of this transcript is available at SWWEC and the RA archives at Woolwich.)
16. SWWEC, Acc. No. 2001-1141, transcript of interview by Dr Peter Liddle with the Right Honourable Sir Robin Dunn, tape 1500, July 2002, p. 11.
17. TNA, WO 171/969, War Diary 7th Field Regiment RA June 1944, Account by Major R. W. D. Dunn MC, RA, pp. 20–1.
18. Ibid., p. 22.
19. SWWEC, Acc. No. 2001-1141, transcript of interview by Dr Peter Liddle with the Right Honourable Sir Robin Dunn, tape 1500, July 2002, p. 13.
20. Ibid.
21. TNA, WO 373/49/608, Recommendation for MC: 74561 Capt. T/Major Robin Horace Walford Dunn (RA), passed by I Corps 4 October 1944.
22. SWWEC, Acc. No. 2001-1141, transcript of interview by Dr Peter Liddle with the Right Honourable Sir Robin Dunn, tape 1500, July 2002, p. 16.

Chapter 2

An 'Instrument Basher' in Britain and the Far East – Albert William Bennett

To become airborne pilots relied on the efforts of several non-flying personnel, particularly those ground crew responsible for maintaining and servicing their aircraft. All airmen and airwomen who enlisted in the wartime RAF or Women's Auxiliary Air Force (WAAF) were allotted a trade within one of six trade groups. These were arranged to reflect the level of responsibility and technical competency required and rates of pay varied according to rank and which trade group an individual belonged. Albert Bennett served as an instrument repairer, a job that may have lacked the glamour associated with aircrew but was nonetheless vital to the operational effectiveness of the RAF both at home and overseas.

Albert was born in October 1914 and grew up in Rochester, Kent. His father was one of the 'Old Contemptibles' (the name adopted by British regular soldiers in France 1914, after the Kaiser reputably described them as a contemptible little army) and spent much of the First World War as a POW. On the outbreak of the Second World War Albert was still living in Rochester and had a managerial position with a firm of office machine and equipment suppliers. As his firm was responsible for maintaining office equipment at police stations, council buildings, hospitals and other establishments vital to the infrastructure of the Home Front in Kent, his job was classed as a reserved occupation.

However, once an older replacement could be found, the 25-year-old Albert was free to enlist in the RAF. He went to a recruiting office in Kidbrooke and was rapidly dispatched to RAF Cardington near Bedford to be kitted out with his uniform and personal equipment. Subsequently, he undertook basic training at an Initial Training Wing (ITW) in Great Yarmouth. This involved extensive drill and weapon training but frequently work was interrupted by air raids.

Later he received technical training at RAF Melksham, Wiltshire:

> I discovered that contrary to the general tales circulating at that time that recruits were being given all the wrong jobs in the service to that in which they had been involved in 'civvy street,' on this course there were in the main office machine engineers and watch repairers, quite appropriate for dealing with the servicing and repair of aircraft instruments.[1]

While there was the occasional misfit, the bulk of recruits had the above technical background and Albert was pleased to be accepted as an 'instrument basher', as they were known within the service.

Having successfully passed the first phase of his trade training he was posted to Central Gunnery School (CGS) at Sutton Bridge, Lincolnshire. Here he was tasked with servicing Supermarine Spitfires and Vickers Wellingtons flown by aircrew who were on refresher courses, very often entailing mock dog fights over the Wash and providing Albert with a significant workload. Additionally, he had to undertake his share of night guard duties overshadowed by ghostly noises, 'probably due to the expansion and contraction of the aircraft fabric and bodywork'.[2]

From Sutton Bridge he was posted back to Melksham for further trade training. He passed this which entitled him to promotion to leading aircraft man, equivalent to a lance corporal in the Army. He was posted back to the CGS and made responsible for maintaining the instruments on no less than twenty-two Westland Lysander aircraft. This had been designed as an Army co-operation aircraft but experience garnered during 1939–40 demonstrated that its slow speed was a severe handicap, particularly when air superiority had not been gained. Consequently, during 1941 the Lysander was replaced in front-line squadrons by the Curtiss P-40 Tomahawk. However, it continued to serve in other roles including air–sea rescue and supporting resistance networks in occupied Europe, where its ability to take off and land in small fields was a decided asset.[3]

At the CGS the Lysander was deployed as a target tug over the Wash using a 'drogue', a wind-sock-like device, that was towed behind the aircraft for other personnel to practise firing at. Albert recalled that while waiting for aircraft to return from exercises ground crew participated in countless games of darts, which was where he first learnt to play that game.

Servicing the Lysander was comparatively straightforward and concentrated on six instruments: altimeter; artificial horizon; wind-speed indicator; temperature gauge; air-speed indicator; and engine 'revs' counter.

The latter could be problematic as:

> the route for the cable (which was encased in an outer casing) was in
> the nature of a double 'S' bend behind the instrument panel and unless
> the outer-casing for this cable was well packed with thick grease, the
> fluctuation on the needle pointer was unbelievable. This needed
> attention after almost every flight of the aircraft.[4]

In his civilian job Albert had been a something of a perfectionist but this
character trait was to land him in trouble in the services. At Sutton Bridge he
was hauled before the station commander, 'up on the carpet' as the RAF
termed it, because he had decided to re-paint some of the panels on the
Lysander aircraft in his care as they appeared scruffy.

> I decided that I would try and improve them and smarten them up with
> some matt black paint. This however turned out to be 'a mortal sin' and
> almost a criminal offence one would have thought, as the pilots
> preferred them in the old and 'tatty' and worn condition and I had to
> try and restore them to this and undo my well intentioned handiwork.[5]

After Sutton Bridge Albert was posted to another section of the CGS at
Cat Foss, Yorkshire where he worked on servicing the instruments on the
Beaufighter aircraft. This was a powerful, twin-engined, heavily armed
monoplane of virtually all-metal construction, the design of which owed
much to improvisation by the Bristol Aircraft Company. In particular, it earned
a fearsome reputation as a long-range and anti-shipping strike fighter when
deployed by Fighter and Coastal Command.[6]

While at Cat Foss Albert was notified that he was due to be posted
overseas. After a brief spell of home leave, he was sent to Blackpool where
like most seaside resorts the boarding houses had been commandeered as
billets by the services. He and his comrades were 'kitted out' with tropical
uniforms and bush hats, which rather negated any efforts at keeping their
destination secret. As Albert stated, it was 'hardly apparel for anywhere else
but "it ain't arf hot mum"'.[7]

From Blackpool he was transported to Liverpool where he boarded the
SS *Stratheden*, a P&O vessel now deployed as a troopship. It sailed via the
Suez Canal in the wake of a minesweeper and eventually docked at Bombay
(Mumbai). Albert had been posted to 322 Maintenance Unit at Cawnpore.
This necessitated a sweltering and tedious journey in an ancient and rickety
train during which Albert awoke at night to discover cockroaches crawling all
over his feet.

Work at 322 Maintenance Unit centred on servicing aircraft that were deployed in supporting the Burma Campaign. Mostly, these were Hawker Hurricane fighters and the Douglas Dakota transport aircraft, a militarised version of the DC-3 commercial airliner. The latter had frequently been deployed to carry mules and 'With the temperature 120 degrees plus, working in the nose of a Dakota was somewhat exhausting and if the aircraft had been carrying mules, often somewhat overpowering.'[8]

The doughty Hawker Hurricane was one of the many aircraft types that Albert worked on during his RAF service. This is a restored example at an air display in Britain. (Robert Goulty)

By 1943, when Albert arrived in theatre, the tide had started to turn against the Japanese. At the end of that year South East Asia Command (SEAC) could muster over 1,000 aircraft, many of which were modern types such as the Hurricane and Spitfire, whereas the enemy had approximately 750 aircraft, about half of which were obsolete. Arrangements were made to construct the necessary airfields to support SEAC operations and with this came an increased demand for logistical and maintenance support.

At Cawnpore work continued with aircraft being serviced in factory like hangars, much in the style of a production line back in Britain. Albert was seconded to the Air Inspection Service, a wartime version of the civilian Air Inspection Directorate. This consisted of a squadron leader as the CO and servicemen selected from all the relevant trades.

Albert's task was to review the servicing of the instruments, mainly on Hurricanes, and ensure that everything was done correctly. He recalled 'the engines being "revved up" and tested with an "erk" [RAF slang for airmen below the rank of corporal] sitting on each side of the tailplane of the Hurricane to keep it on the ground – not a happy experience'.[9] His brief included the maintenance of oxygen equipment and on larger aircraft he had to check the automatic pilot system known as 'George' on British types.

Again, being a perfectionist caused problems and he incurred the displeasure of his flight sergeant by 'being a bit too thorough in my inspections, particularly . . . in respect of "rusty" grid wires on compasses and "pitot-heads" (air speed) not being tight enough'.[10] However, when his superiors learned of his civilian background he was allocated a small workshop and in his spare time tasked with maintaining the unit typewriters. This important role necessitated several trips into the back alleys of Cawnpore in search of spare parts that could be obtained from the locals.

The climate at Cawnpore was unforgiving and the Air Ministry stipulated that after six months' service personnel should be rested at a cooler place in the hills. Consequently, Albert was posted on leave to a hill camp at Chakrata. It was accessed via a steep, winding road negotiated at hair-raising speeds by Indian drivers who seemed oblivious to the drops on either side. He was extremely relieved to arrive at the camp in one piece after such a journey.

His stay ay Chakrata was short-lived as after a few days he was summoned to join 7017 Servicing Echelon supporting No. 155 Squadron in Burma. They had flown the Curtiss P-36 Mohawk before being re-equipped with the Spitfire Mk VIII during January–February 1944, which gave them a decided morale boost. Initially, the squadron had taken a defensive stance but as the war in the Far East progressed and the threat of the Japanese air force diminished they were increasingly deployed on offensive patrols and escort and ground-attack sorties.

Arriving back at Cawnpore Albert was told to report to the squadron at Thedaw, Burma, a journey that would require him to stay in a transit camp near Calcutta. While there he had a stroke of luck:

going up to the ablutions for a wash one evening I got talking to the only other occupant there and it turned out that I was to be his replacement with 155 Squadron as he was on his way home to England. A remarkable and most fortunate coincidence if ever there was one as I learned from him in the course of the conversation that the squadron had indeed left the place that I was posted to, Thedaw, several weeks previously and was in fact making its way down towards Rangoon.[11]

Albert's war continued in the draining climatic conditions of Burma as he and his comrades in the ground crew strove to keep the Spitfires flying. Their work might have lacked the prestige given to most aircrew, but without them No. 155 Squadron would have been wholly ineffective. Typically, a close, respectful bond developed between pilots and the erks of the ground crew, particularly in operational units such as Albert's.

The squadron operated extensively in the Imphal valley and would eventually reach Rangoon in time to witness the Japanese surrender in August 1945. In fact, some of their aircraft escorted the Japanese envoys sent over from Saigon to sign the surrender documents. Albert recalled seeing the Spitfires fly overhead on this momentous occasion as Mingaladone (Rangoon) airfield played its part in the 'short, businesslike and dignified ceremony'.[12]

Shortly after VJ-Day, No. 155 Squadron were tasked with taking part in the re-occupation of Singapore. This required the Spitfires to make the mammoth journey by air from Rangoon. Albert recalled that soon they were involved in evacuating POWs from the notorious Changi prison:

> This was an experience I shall never forget and memories of the release of these men and their appalling condition will always remain with me. Being something of a sentimentalist I still like to imagine that somewhere in Australia there is an Aussie whom I helped and whilst getting him to the transport plane he fell and cut his knee which I then bound up with my handkerchief, and that he may still have that handkerchief as a 'memento' of that day he was released from Changi.[13]

Life in Singapore was comparatively reasonable after the surrender and Albert was amazed at how quickly the shops began to fill up with stock again. It transpired that most of their goods had been hidden away during the Japanese occupation and were now swiftly brought out to supply peacetime consumers. Sadly, he also remembered having to form part of a firing party at the funeral of airmen who had drunk from supplies of Saki that had been poisoned by the Japanese.

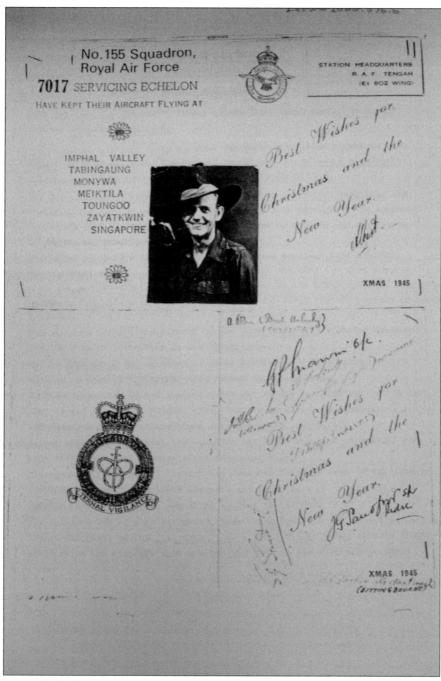

A facsimile of a Christmas card with an attached photograph of Albert Bennett from 1945. Note at the top left that all the places in the Far East where his unit was stationed are listed. (SWWEC)

As an instrument repairer his skills were still much in demand by the post-war RAF because there were relatively few personnel qualified in his trade. Consequently, there appeared to be no immediate prospect of being demobilised and sent home from Singapore. Then, shortly after Christmas 1945, he boarded the *Wuseuh*, a hospital ship that was to transport him and other ground crew to the island of Sumatra.

Although the Second World War had ended, hopes of peace quickly evaporated in the Far East as independence movements seized upon the fall of Japan to advance their causes. In 1946 the RAF were charged with helping to counter a volatile situation in the Dutch East Indies (Indonesia) where separatists sought to take control. Another vital and immediate task was the location and evacuation of former POWs and civilian internees, many of whom had been imprisoned by the Japanese at camps across the Dutch East Indies.

Albert disembarked at Belawan and was then taken in a convoy with an armoured escort to Medan on the north of the island where No. 155 Squadron was based. Here they were responsible for protecting Dutch settlers, many of whom worked as rubber planters, and conducting reconnaissance sorties against the Indonesian separatists.

While on Sumatra he was to have two particularly disturbing experiences. One night members of a 'head hunting' tribe attacked a Direction Finding Post killing all five airmen who manned it, 'slashing the tent where they were to pieces, a terrible sight'.[14] Secondly, Albert was part of search party dispatched to find two missing Spitfire pilots who had suffered a mid-air collision. One bailed out and survived rough in the jungle before making it back to base, but the other was discovered 'dead in his burnt out aircraft and in such a position in the cockpit that it was assumed he was prevented from getting out by terrorists'.[15]

A further problem was that locals employed as daytime labourers would often come back at night to steal supplies from the airfield, especially petrol. As few replacements were coming out from Britain, ground crew were forced to conduct their servicing work and then help guard the airfield at night. Under these trying conditions Albert was promoted corporal in charge of the instruments section.

Eventually, in July 1946 his documents arrived allowing him to return to Britain and be demobilised. With relief he left Medan and took a landing craft back to Singapore from where he was transported home aboard the *Monarch of Bermuda* via Suez. At Liverpool he 'disembarked without any ceremony' and was demobbed the following October, his squadron having already been disbanded.[16]

With his war service behind him he returned to his former trade dealing with office machines and equipment. He remained in that line of business throughout his career, during an era that preceded the advent of the micro computer which replaced the typewriter. He held several managerial posts and on his retirement in 1980 was made chairman of the newly formed Kent Training Group which represented all the Office Machines and Equipment Federation companies in Kent.

In August 1995 he was proud to participate in a march in London commemorating the ending of the Second World War, particularly as he was among a group of Burma Star veterans reviewed by the Queen in front of Buckingham Palace. Additionally, he became a keen supporter of the Rainbow Trust, a charity for terminally ill children and their families. In his retirement he presented talks, including one on his war experiences, to various audiences that helped raise funds for that organisation.

Researching Albert W. Bennett

ORBs outlining the movements and activities of No. 155 Squadron can be viewed within AIR 27 at TNA. Be aware that these are on microfilm which requires patience to trawl through and sadly the reproductive quality is not always as good as it might be. Additionally, they concentrate more on the role of aircrew than the erks servicing aircraft. Records for the CGS can be found within AIR 29 and these contain numerous contemporary photographs, some of which may be of interest from a family history perspective, together with technical reports. To provide a flavour of the latter AIR 29/605 includes information on a 'Revised mounting for 12 bore shot gun in Frazer Nash & Boulton turrets'.

Details of Albert's life and wartime experiences came from a series of documents that he deposited at the SWWEC, and these can be viewed in their archives. The material includes: 'Memories of the RAF & SEAC', a six-page memoir, and the accompanying 'A Sequel to Life in Uniform-RAF Commencing 1946', which outlines his post-war career in the office machines and equipment business. Correspondence between Albert and Mr M. Goodman dated March 1999 further outlines his war service, particularly at Cawnpore. His file includes a facsimile of the 'newspaper' *Rangoon Liberator* dated 27 August 1945 that leads with an article on the Japanese surrender, plus several notes dealing with No. 155 Squadron's Far Eastern experience *c.* 1942–6. These highlight the deployment of the Mohawk and Spitfire by that unit and provide a taste of the sort of combat experienced by the pilots who Albert supported.

Albert, like many servicemen of his generation, had to endure troopships or the equivalent to reach far-flung destinations such as Cawnpore. Colonel H. C. B. Rodgers, OBE, *Troopships and their History* (London, 1963) is a useful guide to these vessels including many deployed during 1939–45. Good places to hunt for this type of book would be the IWM (Department of Books), London, or second-hand book shops or via inter library loan.

Anyone interested in researching a member of the wartime RAF, perhaps a relative, might wish to consider visiting the RAF Museum at Hendon, London. Not only does it have galleries covering over a hundred years of military aviation, but it also possesses a library and archive service. For up-to-date information, particularly on conducting research at Hendon, please visit: www.rafmuseum.com.

There are three general histories of the RAF that are helpful in outlining the war in the Far East and the role of ground crew: Christopher Chant's *The History of the RAF: From 1939 to the Present* (Regency House Publishing Ltd, 1993); Chaz Bowyer's *The Royal Air Force 1939–1945* (Pen & Sword, 1996); and Air Chief Marshal Sir Michael Armitage's *The Royal Air Force: An Illustrated History* (Brockhampton Press, 1998). The dynamics of the air war in the Far East are further covered by John Buckley in *Air Power in the Age of Total War* (UCL Press, 1999) and David Rooney in *Burma Victory: Imphal to Kohima March 1944 to May 1945* (Cassell & Co. Ltd, 2002). While Max Hastings's *Nemesis: The Battle for Japan, 1944–45* (Harper Press, 2007) provides one of the most recent accounts describing the latter phases of the war in the Far East, including the decisions to drop the atomic bombs on Hiroshima and Nagasaki.

Notes

1. Second World War Experience Centre, Acc. No. 2000.676, 'Memories of the RAF & SEAC' by Albert William Bennett (RAF 1645599), p. 1.
2. Ibid., p. 2.
3. Details of the Westland Lysander can be found in David Mondey's *The Hamlyn Concise Guide to British Aircraft of World War Two* (Chancellor Press, 1995), pp. 227–9.
4. SWWEC, Acc. No. 2000.676, 'Memories of the RAF & SEAC' by Albert William Bennett (RAF 1645599), p. 2.
5. Ibid.
6. Details of the Bristol Beaufighter can be found in Mondey, *The Hamlyn Concise Guide to British Aircraft of World War Two*, pp. 61–7.
7. SWWEC, Acc. No. 2000.676, 'Memories of the RAF & SEAC' by Albert William Bennett (RAF 1645599), p. 2.
8. Ibid., p. 3.
9. SWWEC, Acc. No. 2000.676.2, correspondence between Mr Albert W. Bennett and Mr M. Goodman, 21 March 1999.

10. Ibid.
11. SWWEC, Acc. No. 2000.676, 'Memories of the RAF & SEAC' by Albert William Bennett (RAF 1645599), p. 4.
12. SWWEC, Acc. No. 2000.676.5, Facsimile of: 'Rangoon Liberator Special Edition Monday, August 27 1945', front-page headline.
13. SWWEC, Acc. No. 2000.676, 'Memories of the RAF & SEAC' by Albert William Bennett (RAF 1645599), p. 5.
14. Ibid., p. 6.
15. Ibid.
16. Ibid.

Chapter 3

A Commando's Tale –
Eric De La Torre

During the late 1930s the research section of the General Staff highlighted the possibility of deploying specialised units in raids on enemy territory. After Dunkirk the War Office was persuaded of the viability of this idea and with Churchill's backing the Special Service Brigade was formed. During 1940–2 the Commandos, as they became known, lifted public morale when it was flagging and enhanced their own reputation as an elite force by mounting numerous raids on *Festung Europa*.

However, senior Army officers resented units being denuded of their best men and political wrangling over the Commandos' intended role had to be overcome. Like most of the Army, the Commandos additionally had to operate with a shortage of equipment and resources for training. As the war progressed Commandos increasingly fought alongside regular units rather than as a small specialised raiding force. They still maintained their elite status and often seized critical objectives ahead of conventional troops.

Eric De La Torre was involved with the Commandos almost from their inception. He was born in September 1918 to a mother of Irish extraction and a Spanish father who worked as a City banker. He was educated at John Fisher School in Purley where he was a founder member, there being only twenty-eight other boys when he started. He especially enjoyed cross-country running and cricket which may have been an asset on joining the Army.

At 17 he left school hoping to become a missionary priest and attended a seminary in Liverpool. Here he was told that he could not go into the missions but would be welcome to teach in the seminary owing to his Classics education. This was not to his taste and to the disappointment of his father he left to train as an accountant.

On the outbreak of war he was studying for his accountancy exams and in October 1939 was called up into the Royal Army Ordnance Corps (RAOC).

Commandos storming ashore from their assault craft, possibly on an exercise, demonstrate the original function of these units as an amphibious raiding force. Note the man in the centre armed with a Thompson sub-machine gun, or 'Tommy gun', a weapon synonymous with the Commandos who initially used it in great numbers. (Taylor Library)

He did his basic training at Didcot, Berkshire. Lacking any previous military experience, he discovered he enjoyed the discipline, drill and rifle training which helped him cope with the general 'square bashing'.

Subsequently, he was posted to Number 3 Ordnance Field Park at Ruislip. One day a notice went up on Park Orders requesting volunteers for 'special troops'. Eric felt that this sounded exciting and offered something different from the humdrum of soldiering in a British depot. Consequently, he reported to a group of officers in London who told him that plans were afoot to form a parachute regiment and Commandos for amphibious raiding. Eric leaped at the chance to become a 'para' but was informed he lacked sufficient infantry experience, particularly with small arms. Instead, he was put down for the Commandos.

Shortly afterwards he spent three weeks undertaking physical training at the Guards Barracks in Windsor before being dispatched to Scotland by rail. He was issued with money, a travel warrant and told to wear civilian clothes and carry his uniform in a suitcase. In the Orderly Room at Largs the sergeant asked for his name and then turning to his corporal announced 'Another bloody fool. The body will be washed up on the French coast soon.'[1] Not perhaps the most auspicious start.

The trainees were sent to civilian billets. It was a principle of the Commandos to keep administration to a minimum and encourage soldiers to be resourceful and independent while simultaneously maintaining a high level of military discipline and turnout. Eric was posted to Number 8 Commando and soon embarked on a series of night landings and exercises on the Isle of Arran. Each landing was frequently followed by marches of around 20–30 miles in the pouring rain and in full equipment which was extremely tough.

Commando training was intentionally mentally tough and physically demanding. Here a man is put through his paces in mountainous terrain, probably in Scotland. (Taylor Library)

At this stage Commando training was still in its comparative infancy but the idea was to gear men up for hit and run raids on the enemy coast. Consequently, weapons handling, physical fitness, the ability to move rapidly at night and training in amphibious operations were crucial. As a motivating factor trainees faced the threat of being RTU'd (Returned To Unit) if they failed to come up to standard.

Eric became a wireless operator to Bob Laycock, the CO. Wireless training was done 'on the job' using the Number 18 Set, a short-range man pack radio designed for infantry use. It struggled to cope with hilly terrain as this screened the signal. Consequently, Eric spent many cold hours fruitlessly trying to establish contact with other units on exercises, much to the chagrin of his CO.

After two or three months of tough training he was sent on embarkation leave and went back to his family in Streatham, London. One evening Eric was stepping off the bus during the wartime blackout and missing the curb, he sprained his ankle. On returning to Number 8 Commando, then preparing for the Middle East, he was informed that he could not go with them as he

Commandos training in unarmed combat techniques which heightened aggression and instilled confidence, both of which were vital when on active service. (Taylor Library)

was not fit enough to march. Instead, he was transferred to Number 3 Commando that had moved to Largs. They were about to mount a raid on the Lofoten Islands off the northern coast of Norway (4 March 1941).

Known as Operation Claymore, this proved a success. German prisoners were taken, shipping sunk and fish-oil factories were destroyed which would have provided valuable vitamins for enemy troops. The raid did much to validate the Commando idea. Given his sprained ankle, Eric missed Claymore. However, his first taste of action came when he was involved in Operation Archery (27 December 1941), a major raid against Vaagso and Maaloy Islands, Norway. The raid relied on the increasing competence of the British at combined operations and was the first time the Commandos had been deployed against a defended port.

There were five assault groups. Eric's was tasked with seizing the town of South Vaagso. His job was to act as one of Lieutenant Colonel John Durnford-Slater's (CO Number 3 Commando) wireless operators. This ensured that he might easily come into contact with the enemy. As he explained:

> you didn't know what the Colonel was going to do. How he was going to organise things. Because each Troop had a signaller with the Troop Officer so the officer leading the attack, or whatever it was, he has got his signaller with him and his Commando troop. So the signallers could be very much involved.[2]

The raiders set sail from Britain over the Christmas holidays 1941 and were briefed aboard ship. At Scapa Flow Lord Louis Mountbatten (Chief of Combined Operations) came aboard and inspected them with the following words: 'When you get to Vaagso you will give them hell. They machine-gunned my men in the water when HMS *Kelly* was sunk. I want you to remember that.'[3]

Naval gunfire helped the Commandos ashore. Once there bitter street fighting ensued with elements of the German 181st Division, many of whom were skilled combat veterans. Initially, it was difficult for Eric to know what was happening as he maintained his position aboard the colonel's vessel. Then the stirring sound of bag pipes was heard as the second in command, 'mad' Jack Churchill, led his assault against a German battery on Maaloy.

Approaching the shore, Eric's craft was targeted by a German lorry with a gun mounted on the back, 'a stream of tracer flew over the barge about five feet up and you know it wasn't, it didn't look any more dangerous than fireworks really'.[4] Then the order was given to 'Stand by' and as the landing craft grounded the Commandos stormed ashore.

Eric's first sight was that of a friend rolling around in the snow with his battledress ablaze. Unfortunately, an RAF Hampden bomber supporting the raid by laying a smoke screen had been hit by enemy fire. The stricken aircraft accidentally dropped a phosphorous bomb on a landing craft. Eric ran over to his friend saying, 'Are you alright Wilkie' and Durnford-Slater told him, 'Leave him, you know the orders. The naval ratings will see to him.'[5]

Shortly afterwards news filtered back that Captain Jonny Giles had been killed while street fighting. A giant of a man, who had been a keen boxer and rugby player, he had been leading Number 3 Troop towards South Vaagso. Eric remembered that losing such a good officer so soon seemed to spell trouble. As he and the signals sergeant heard the crash of grenades and gunfire they desperately tried to make contact with the forward troops but failed.

Eric started to climb further up the mountainside to try and obtain better reception. As he did so a bullet whizzed over his head, 'I flattened myself behind the rock and took my helmet off and put my pistol inside and raised it above the rock and then sure enough another bullet flew over.'[6] He did this again and again with the same result. Then carefully he inched his way back down the mountainside. Naval gunfire was brought down on the mountainside but still the signallers had no luck with their sets.

Eventually, the colonel ordered them to pick up sacks of grenades from the beach dump and take them to the Ulvesund Hotel, which had become a German strongpoint. At the hotel Eric witnessed one of the Commando officers in an assault, 'He had a grenade in each hand and he had drawn the pins and the Germans fired through the door and hit him as he arrived there and fell on his own grenades on the front step.'[7]

While the fighting raged Eric and the signal section continued to try and make their equipment function. Simultaneously, they remained ready to engage the Germans if necessary. Then a recall rocket was launched by the Navy, keen to move off rather than risk being attacked by German bombers in a fjord. Eric recalled that everybody returned to their ships:

> taking prisoners and equipment and some Norwegians who wanted to go back . . . I went down to my bunk and there was a young Norwegian woman sitting on my bunk with a little girl about seven or eight years old . . . and both of them looked terrified and all I could think was that, I didn't speak Norwegian, but all I could think is that she was going to join her husband in England perhaps who had joined the Free Norwegians, and fortunately I remembered I had a bar of chocolate in my kit bag . . . and gave it to the little girl.[8]

On the voyage back to Britain a burial was held at sea for some of the Commandos and Germans killed in the raid. 'It was very moving . . . the chaps were standing around still with their bandages on. With our dressings on, which hadn't been attended to yet, and their faces blackened . . .'.[9]

Overall the raid had been a great success and was well executed by all three armed services. The Commandos demonstrated their flare for amphibious warfare. Enemy shipping, fish-oil processing plants and other installations were destroyed. Over 100 Germans were captured and returned to Britain with a handful of Quislings (a term for pro-Nazi sympathisers coined after the infamous collaborator Vidkun Quisling who became the prime minister of Norway under the German occupation) and recruits for the Free Norwegian Army. Crucially, Archery convinced Hitler to maintain a sizeable garrison in Norway to the detriment of the German war effort elsewhere.

Over New Year 1942 the Commandos were given a rousing reception back at Largs. They had given the Germans a bloody nose. Eric then enjoyed some home leave. He discovered that his elder sister had virtually seen as much action as him. She worked as a nurse during the bombing of the East End of London. Returning to the Commandos, he continued training in amphibious warfare techniques with a strong emphasis on physical fitness. He was then selected for a demolition course. Afterwards the CO called the 'students' into his office and asked if they would like to attend a dock demolition course 'with the chance of a bit of fun at the end of it'.[10]

Although Eric did not realise it at the time, this 'fun' referred to Operation Chariot (24 March 1942), an audacious raid against the German naval base at St Nazaire. The French port contained the only Atlantic dry dock able to accept the *Tirpitz*, Germany's last-surviving modern battleship. If this dock, originally built for the ocean liner *Normandie*, could be destroyed it would severely hamper German capabilities in the Atlantic.

Training started at Rosyth. Here the layout of the docks and types of explosive were explained by Captains Montgomery and Pritchard of the Royal Engineers. Eric and his comrades realised something special was afoot. Soon they were posted to the King George V Dock at Southampton and guided around the facilities. Then they were given:

> dummy charges, which would be the same weights as we would carry in action, and we were blindfolded and they had to give us a night time raid on the pumping house and Montgomery timed each team how long they took to get down the iron ladders blindfolded into the basement of the pumping house and place charges on the pillar pumps and then get up again.[11]

Further training took place at Cardiff docks before the men were told to return to their Commando. On the train blinds were drawn. In the morning they were surprised to find to find themselves at Falmouth rather than Largs. Here the demolition teams were briefed together with Number Two Commando which were forming the assault parties.

Most sailed towards St Nazaire in flimsy 'B' class Fairmile boats, a type of motor launch (ML). These were 'built of two thin skins of mahogany, with a lining of calico between, so that they would not resist even a rifle bullet'.[12] They were seaworthy and comparatively fast but hardly suited to the job in hand. Ahead steamed HMS *Campbeltown*, a former American destroyer packed with explosives and converted to appear like a German vessel. She was to ram the southern caisson of the Normandie Dock and transport some of the other demolition teams.

To the front and rear of the flotilla a gun boat and motor torpedo boats (MTBs) provided protection. The idea was that force would be considered 'friendly' by the enemy, a factor assisted by the British possessing the latest German naval codes, and so gain access to the Loire.

Aboard ML 262, Eric tried to pass the time by reading a book. Like his comrades, he was aware that 'not many of us were going to come back, or at least there was a good chance we weren't coming back' because the briefing had shown where 'the coastal batteries were on either bank of the Loire and it looked a very tough job'.[13]

Eric's team, under Lieutenant Woodcock, was to target a bridge at the Old Entrance to the docks. They had to wait for other teams to finish their demolition tasks then the Commandos would escape via the MLs. As the *Campbeltown* hauled down the Swastika and replaced it with the Ensign the flotilla was under a hail of fire. The Germans having realised a raiding party was in their midst used every gun available.

Woodcock offered everyone aboard ML 262 a tot of rum as they prepared to disembark. Unfortunately, ML 192 directly in front was hit and veered across ML 262. The skipper had to take avoiding action. In the confusion he missed the Old Entrance. After sailing up the river he made a second attempt. In the dock a ship fired on them as they landed. As the Commandos ran towards their target Sergeant Headston of the protection party was hit.

Suddenly, someone shouted 'Get down' and 'we flung ourselves on the ground and the winding house for the dock gates went up'.[14] One of the demolition teams aboard *Campbeltown* had gone ashore and done its business. Together with another sergeant, Eric tried to retrieve Headston and recall ML 262.

It was chaos aboard. Woodcock told Eric to go below whereupon he:

> saw three men lying across the mess deck table. I didn't know whether
> they were . . . they weren't moving at all and I concluded they were dead
> because bullets were coming through one side . . . and out the other side
> . . . I thought 'God I am not staying down here. I will be safer on deck'.[15]

On deck he encountered Lieutenant Smalley who had led the attack on the
winding house. Smalley ran forward to man the Oerlikon despite warnings
that it was out of action. Suddenly, 'his head appeared to have gone, and
there was this headless figure with these shoulder pads [for the gun] . . .
and Smalley's head rolling across the deck and I think it was the recoil that
did it'.[16] Shortly afterwards the skipper gave the order to 'abandon boat' as
ML 262 suffered a direct hit.

Another shell crashed through the bridge. Woodcock fell onto Eric who
shook him a couple of times without response. Then:

> we all went overboard and I went down about seven or eight feet . . .
> I had a pistol in each pocket . . . we had all been told to inflate our Mae
> Wests [life jackets] . . . under our battledress jackets and as I came to
> the surface a shell . . . went into the side of the boat.[17]

The shell didn't explode owing to its wooden construction. Eric was floating
down the Loire amidst pools of burning fuel and the shattered remains of
several MLs. A sailor's voice rang out 'Oh God Help in Ages Past' amidst the
chaos. Eric could see figures on the shore and hoped they were French.
However, as they floated closer he recognised their distinctive 'coal-scuttle'
German helmets. He was hauled out of the water by a party of German
Marines. In perfect English their officer said, 'Which are your wounded?' They
had been tracking the raiders down the Loire. Eric handed over his pistol to
a youthful-looking German. The German then took off his signet ring with a
coat of arms of St Nazaire and handed it over to Eric as a souvenir.

Eric spent several weeks in a transit camp near Hamburg. Officers and
men were then separated and he was sent to the notorious Stalag at
Lamsdorf. Typically, this suffered from overcrowding, poor sanitation and had
'the atmosphere of a European seaport city, with a good deal of the spit-and-
polish of the regular British Army superimposed'.[18]

As he was not an officer Eric was expected to work. Together with other
captured Commandos he was sent to Stermberg on the border with
Czechoslovakia. They were tasked with making wooden huts for bombed out
civilians. This presented Eric with his first chance to escape. With another

Commando he crossed the border one night but was caught eight days later at a road block. He received seven days with only bread and water as punishment.

Another chance of escape came when Eric was detailed to a forestry job where it was impossible for the guards to keep watch over everyone simultaneously. With a young soldier who had been captured at Dunkirk, he set off through the woods. Subsequently, they sought shelter in a German goods train but were spotted by a worker who alerted the military. As dawn approached they desperately hid in blackberry bushes only to be discovered by some children. The 'next thing we saw was a couple of German jackboots' and a soldier with his revolver drawn told them to 'come out'. This time he received 'fourteen days bread and water at a German military prison'.[19]

Along with other troublemakers, Eric was locked up in a camp full of Russian prisoners. He had his boots and braces removed to prevent future escapes. One night 'we heard a scratching on the wall and we thought "God, rats they must be," and a knot hole in the woodwork was through and a beam of light came through from next door, and I looked through and in the light I saw another eye.'[20] This was the senior Russian prisoner who told them a British doctor would be visiting the camp.

Unfortunately, the doctor refused to do anything for them as technically nothing medically was wrong. Eric was then transported to a sugar-beet factory near Ratibor where several other British POWs worked. Conditions were tough. The night shift was from 6pm until 6am with men washing beet out of railway wagons. Prisoners tried to steal sugar but soon the Germans got wise to this. Sometimes, train loads of German wounded would pull up at an adjacent siding and the POWs refilled their water bottles. Simultaneously, they took the opportunity to sabotage the wagons covertly by putting sand in their oil boxes.

The factory foreman had a small hut with a bed in it that was kept unlocked. Secretly several POWs used to creep in for a sleep. Eric was caught doing this. As punishment he was sent to spend a night shovelling lime at a factory manned by Russian POWs. His mask was filthy and he couldn't breathe. He complained to a guard who drew his pistol, pointed it at his stomach and said 'Shovel'. Then other prisoners 'heard the commotion. And there was this big Russian I used to give cigarettes to, a very nice chap . . . very emaciated . . . poor fellow because they didn't get any of the sort of food that we got'.[21] The Russian and two of Eric's Commando friends stood watching. All were 'armed' with shovels and fortunately the German thought better of it and stopped bullying Eric.

Shortly afterwards Eric was dispatched to a limestone quarry for troublesome prisoners. It was extremely tough, especially for POWs who were not in top physical shape. The Germans made the prisoners stay until they had done twelve skips. Then they were marched back to camp so exhausted that it was usually an hour before they felt up to eating anything.

After a month a British doctor managed to persuade the Germans that Eric had TB. He was sent back to Lamsdorf where he ended up in the repatriation compound. Here he received extra Red Cross parcels. Eventually, the Germans decided he should be sent to a convalescent compound instead.

It was now the winter of 1944–5 and POWs were being moved from the camp. Eric and others decided to hide away in the now-empty NCOs' compound and await liberation. They survived on potatoes and by burning wooden bunks to keep warm. The Germans came back to move the camp hospital, found the miscreant POWs and locked them on a train bound for the West.

They ended up under canvas outside Memmingen, Bavaria. It was very cold and 'we used to pool our blankets, and we were lying on straw and we made a bed. There were twelve of you in it so we were all in blankets and we would take it in turns to be the two on the outside, and if you get enough bodies together you can keep warm'.[22]

Tiring of the conditions, Eric and a comrade decided to escape. With the war nearly over, they bribed the driver of the truck that delivered potatoes to the camp to take them into town. He wanted 200 cigarettes and between them the POWs managed to pay up. Another two battledress-clad figures wandering around Memmingen made little difference as slave labourers and various people where wearing it by mid-1945.

Eric and his friend stayed in a hotel, having persuaded the proprietor that they would put in a 'good word' for him when liberation came. After a week there was an announcement over a loud speaker that the Americans would soon be coming. A 'Sherman tank came through the gate . . . flanked by infantry and the tank drew level with us and the commander said "You guys English," and we said "Yes." "Come and have a ride."'[23]

Eric was flown back to Britain and eventually given an uninspiring desk job at Woolwich. He managed to rejoin the Commandos hoping to see action in the Far East. However, they were disbanded and he was demobbed. After his wartime experiences he felt unable to resume studying accountancy. Luckily, a friend from the RAOC asked if he was interested in going into business.

The two of them opened a sports shop in Harlesden, North London with some success. Later he married and had a family. He remained in contact with many wartime comrades and in 1946 was a founder member of the Commando St Nazaire Society. He was later awarded the MBE for his services to that organisation and has appeared on television talking about his wartime service.

Researching Eric De La Torre

The basis for this chapter was the October 2002 interview with Eric De La Torre conducted by David Talbot on behalf of the SWWEC. Transcripts of tapes 1665 and 1666 are available at their archives. These provide details of his background, personal wartime experience, and what happened to him on demob. The SWWEC and IWM Sound Archive also hold the personal testimony of other wartime Commandos, including individuals involved in Operation Chariot.

Eric appeared as an interviewee in the Channel 4 series *COMMANDO* (2002) and BBC documentary *Greatest Raid of all Time* (2007) about Operation Chariot. Both provide useful if brief insights that helped outline his wartime experience with the Commandos. If you use an Internet search engine several sites dealing with the Commandos will crop up, but be warned that web content is unedited and needs to be treated with care.

TNA contain numerous documents dealing with the Commandos. War Diaries for No. 8 and No. 3 Commando, in which Eric served, covering 1940–2 are in WO 218. These are official operational records and seldom give specific details on individual soldiers. However, generally they do provide information on training and operations that may help to piece together an individual's wartime service or at least put it into context. Typically, entries in those for the Commandos are brief as befitting of an organisation that did not welcome overmuch administration.

Operations Archery and Chariot are covered by reports in WO 231, WO 106 and WO 361, the latter including information on missing Commandos. However, bear in mind that as the Commandos fought within a combined operations framework it is worth looking beyond the War Office papers and at those for the Admiralty and Air Ministry. Operation Archery is covered within ADM 1 and AIR 20, while information on Operation Chariot can be found in ADM 1, AIR 8, AIR 14 and AIR 15. These will not yield genealogical information but offer a clear impression of the operational challenges that had to be surmounted.

For anyone like Eric who was captured it is worth checking WO 344 Directorate of Military Intelligence Liberated POW Questionnaires. These give basic personal information and detail on aspects of POW life such as camps, medical treatment, work details, escapes and punishments received. On liberation Eric raided the filing cabinet in his camp's office containing his German POW records and later passed these onto his youngest son. It is always worth checking if any similar personal documents survive within your own family when you are trying to research a relative's wartime past. Adrian Gilbert's *POW Allied Prisoners in Europe 1939–1945* (John Murray, 2007) is a well-researched, accessible and vivid account relating the experience of Allied servicemen captured by the Germans and Italians.

James D. Ladd's *Commandos and Rangers of World War II* (Book Club Associates, 1978) provides a useful general source on the formation, training and operational experience of the Commandos. While an article by the same author, 'Preparing for Action: Commando Weapons and Training 1940–45' in *The Elite Against All Odds Magazine,* Vol. 4 (Orbis Publishing Ltd, 1985), gives helpful detail on weapons and equipment.

Similarly, Simon Dunstan's *Commandos Churchill's 'Hand of Steel'* (Ian Allen Publishing, 2003) summarises wartime operations, provides information on equipment and outlines the careers of some of the main Commando personalities. Another generic work that is useful on the doctrine, training, organisation and combat experience of the Commandos is Tim Moreman's *Osprey Battle Orders No. 18 British Commandos 1940–46* (Osprey Publishing, 2006).

The late Brigadier Peter Young DSO, MC and bars wrote widely on military history including the Commandos in which he served. His articles on Operation Archery, 'The First Commando Raids' in *Purnell's History of the Second World War* (Phoebus Publishing Ltd, 1967), Vol. 2, No. 15 and 'Blooding the Commandos: No. 3 Commando Vaagso' in *The Elite Against All Odds Magazine,* Vol. 3 (Orbis Publishing Ltd, 1985), cover salient points regarding that raid. Both are well illustrated and benefit from the author's personal experience.

There are numerous accounts of Operation Chariot and the most widely available are mentioned here. C. E. Lucas Phillips's *The Greatest Raid of All* (Pan Books, 2000) provides the classic account of the operation and was originally published in 1958. Lucas Phillips, another distinguished soldier who later became well known for his gardening books, lends his professional insight into the military problems that faced the Commandos. Despite its age, the book is an ideal starting point for those interested in the raid on St Nazaire and who may wish to research an individual or unit that was involved in it.

Jon Cooksey's *Operation Chariot: The Raid on St Nazaire* (Pen & Sword, 2005) is a highly readable narrative of the raid and supplements *The Greatest Raid of All*. It employs several helpful illustrations and relies on the personal testimony of participants. Similarly, James Dorrian's *Saint Nazaire Operation Chariot – 1942* (Pen & Sword, 2006) is a handy guide book for those wishing to visit the area today. It is interlaced with veteran's memories and contains useful diagrams and photographs. The graphic showing the conversion of HMS *Campbeltown* to resemble a twin-funnelled German destroyer is particularly good. Ken Ford's *Osprey Campaign No. 92 St Nazaire 1942: The Great Commando Raid* (Osprey Publishing, 2008) is another well-illustrated and accessible book that provides the reader with a clear outline of the operation.

Notes

1. Second World War Experience Centre, transcript of tape 1665, Mr E. De La Torre interviewed by David Talbot, 24 October 2002, p. 5.
2. Ibid., p. 8.
3. Ibid., p. 7.
4. Ibid., p. 9.
5. Ibid.
6. Ibid.
7. Ibid., p. 10.
8. Ibid.
9. Ibid.
10. Ibid., p. 12.
11. Ibid.
12. C. E. Lucas Phillips, *The Greatest Raid of All* (Pan Books, 2000), p. 72.
13. SWWEC, transcript of tape 1665, Mr E. De La Torre interviewed by David Talbot, 24 October 2002, p. 14.
14. Ibid., pp. 14–15.
15. Ibid., p. 15.
16. Ibid.
17. Ibid.
18. New Zealand official POW history quoted in Adrian Gilbert, *POW Allied Prisoners in Europe 1939–1945* (John Murray, 2007), p. 85.
19. SWWEC, transcript of tape 1665, Mr E. De La Torre interviewed by David Talbot, 24 October 2002, pp. 19–20.
20. Ibid., p. 20.
21. Ibid., p. 23.
22. Ibid., p. 25.
23. Ibid., p. 26.

Chapter 4

Bomb Disposal and Mine Clearance with the Wartime Royal Navy – the Revd C. Bert Blackmore

Bert Blackmore was born in Northern Ireland in 1917, although his branch of the family had originated in Devon where they ran fishing boats out of Brixham. Several members of his family including his father had served in the Navy. However, by the time Bert was born his father had left the service and held a position with the Surveyor's Department of the Board of Trade in Londonderry, part of which entailed inspecting ships.

He was educated at a local church school that brought pupils from primary grade right through to Northern Ireland School Certificate level. Bert had an active social life and was heavily involved in the Church. In 1933 his family moved to Hull as the Board of Trade's activities were transferred there. Here he continued his education at a local business college before joining an engineering supplies firm as a secretary.

On the outbreak of war Bert determined to join the Navy and in January 1940 had his medical. Afterwards he was informed that the Navy currently had few vacancies for new recruits. Consequently, it was five months before he was called up to go to HMS *Collingwood*, a training base near Portsmouth that had been planned before the war and only recently opened. Here recruits received their first taste of the naval culture that was to surround them throughout their service.

Bert recalled that Collingwood:

was really a collection of wooden huts, . . . we were . . . allocated to one of the huts and then the following day we were kitted out and looked like sailors whether we were or not. For the first five weeks of our training we were on the parade ground. It was all drill, drill, drill day after day . . . we had full sized dummy rifles that we did rifle drill and all the rest with.[1]

Having been drilled extensively in the Church Lads Brigade as a boy he found the 'square bashing' comparatively easy to cope with. However, he was surprised by its duration as an introduction to other subjects, including seamanship, did not commence until the five weeks had elapsed. The initial phase of a seaman's career was all about discipline and, as one historian noted, 'the training syllabus included practically no contact with real naval ships'.[2]

Eventually, Bert received instruction in basic seamanship and naval gunnery at Collingwood using guns left over from the First World War. During the final week of his basic training his contingent were memorably inspected by King George VI. Subsequently, they were posted to Portsmouth Barracks at the height of the Battle of Britain when air raids and invasion scares were an all-pervading part of life for service personnel and civilians alike.

Bert and some of those men he had joined up with from Hull soon discovered that drafts were being sent to HMS *King George V*, a 35,000-ton battleship. They did not fancy this and hung back so they could be drafted to HMS *Jersey*, a 'J' or Javelin class destroyer then refitting in Hull. She was a

A wartime portrait of a youthful Bert Blackmore, possibly taken at the time he joined HMS Jersey. (SWWEC)

comparatively modern ship having entered service in the late 1930s and distinctively had only one funnel as she required fewer boilers than many older vessels. *Jersey* would eventually serve in the Mediterranean where like most of the 'J' class she endured a torrid time and was eventually mined off Malta in 1941.[3]

On joining *Jersey* Bert and the crew were involved in two weeks of hectic preparations prior to assembling with Lord Mountbatten's flotilla at Devonport. En route they stopped in the Thames Estuary to serve as escort for the monitor HMS *Erebus* and several minesweeping vessels and merchant ships.

Everything went well until one of the minesweepers hit a mine and was sunk. When another minesweeper went to help it too was mined. Bert remembered that the *Jersey* lowered one of her boats to mount a rescue and the crew had a close shave. A mine 'came up just . . ., beside us, or at least . . . the mine didn't actually come up, they were all magnetic, . . . and it exploded . . . on our starboard bow', luckily causing no casualties.[4] However, the *Jersey* did have to go into dry dock in London for repairs after this incident.

Bert was part of the crew that stayed with the ship at West India Docks during the Blitz. She was never in danger during the heavy bombing of the East End but a piece of shrapnel did once strike him on his helmet. When the repairs were completed the *Jersey* joined her flotilla and patrolled the Channel and Western Approaches.

German destroyers were known to be based at Brest and soon the *Jersey* became involved in an encounter with them. Bert had an ordinary seaman's eye view of the action as the cartridge man in one of the *Jersey*'s turrets that mounted twin 4.7in guns. His job was to put cartridges onto a tray prior to them being loaded into the breech.

> It was quite a fierce engagement while it lasted. It wasn't a long one, round about twenty minutes, half an hour, but it was, it was quite fierce and it wasn't particularly pleasant listening to shells flying overhead. . . . it was an interesting experience . . . I wasn't afraid. Apprehensive a little bit probably, . . . my main fear of it, if there was a fear, was that I would let the side down.[5]

Shortly afterwards the *Jersey* was ordered to the Mediterranean as escort for 'Force H', the Navy's Gibraltar-based task force that included the capital ships HMS *Renown* and aircraft carrier HMS *Ark Royal*. They were involved in the bombardment of Genoa but for much of their tour life was fairly routine for the crew.

Later the *Jersey* was dispatched to patrol home waters, particularly around the Bristol Channel area before embarking on another deployment with 'Force

H'. During this deployment the hunt for the *Bismarck* occurred and the *Jersey* had to escort the larger ships on a lengthy voyage as they formed up to cover 'the southern end of the chase, of the hunt'.[6]

The weather was appalling but under such conditions life on board was manageable.'The living space, quarters, are small, are compact [on a destroyer] . . . there were no bunks or anything like that, you slept in hammocks, and it's the most comfortable sleep you could possibly have is in a hammock. Especially on a ship that's rolling.'[7]

The *Jersey* was then tasked with escorting the damaged HMS *Resolution*, a Royal Sovereign class battleship of First World War vintage, back from the Mediterranean. On returning to Britain, Bert left the ship as he had been selected for a commission. However, while at Portsmouth barracks awaiting his Admiralty selection board he was wounded during an air raid:

> I was on fire watch duty in the roof space of one of the barrack blocks and a land mine fell on the end of the building . . . we had had several incendiary mines through and . . . we had deal with those and I was walking down to the end, . . . of the building to see if there's anything come through there when the whole end of the building just went up in a flash, . . . I was blown back onto my back and I didn't realise at the time that . . ., a lot of the glass from one of the skylights had gone into my face and made a horrible mess of it.[8]

Consequently, he was hospitalised for nine weeks but the medics did a tremendous job. When he had fully recovered he was only left with a scar behind one of his ears. Bert was then sent to HMS *King Alfred*, a former leisure complex at Hove that had been commandeered by the Navy, initially to train reservists and later potential officers.

Having passed his officer training and been commissioned into the Royal Naval Volunteer Reserve (RNVR), he attended an address by an officer on behalf of the Director of Unexploded Bombs Department (UXB Department). He volunteered for service with that organization, although at the time he didn't entirely appreciate what he was letting himself in for.

Just three mornings of training at Chatham on the handling and use of explosives served as his introduction to the 'world' of naval bomb disposal. Subsequently, Bert was able to receive instruction from a bomb disposal officer at Immingham who had valuable first-hand experience and knowledge to pass on. Additionally, he attended a brief course on fuses at HMS *Vernon*, the RN torpedo training school at Portsmouth.

Despite the brevity of the above training he picked up some useful tips from his instructors. However, ultimately there was no substitute for gaining on-the-job experience by dealing with genuine UXBs. As the war progressed his remit was extended to included not just bombs but mine clearance and disposal as well.

After spending a few months working in Belfast Bert was posted to take charge of bomb disposal on Tyneside. Routinely mines had to be defused, ideally at safe distance from populated areas. Ships that had been bombed required examination and reports on this work were regularly sent to the Admiralty.

A cargo of oranges from Spain presented a particularly unusual challenge. Small explosive devices had been hidden among the cargo and one blew up en route, while another had to be made safe by Bert's team when the ship docked. It was possible that enemy agents or Spaniards with pro-German sympathies had placed these charges on board with the aim of sinking the ship and its morale-boosting cargo.

Tragically, in the Newcastle area Bert was to witness the only fatality that was suffered by the local bomb disposal unit when under his command. They were dealing with a mine on a beach below a cliff that couldn't be blown up in situ. Therefore, it was defused and arrangements made to remove it.

> We rigged the sheer legs [a structure usually comprising two upright spars, joined at the top to form a triangle, with a hoisting tackle suspended at the apex, and capable of lifting heavy weights]. The petty officer and myself went down again. We connected the mine to the sheer legs . . . and it was hauled by those on top [of the cliff] . . . and as it came up it began to wobble a bit and the sheer legs collapsed . . . But it collapsed inwards and the petty officer, who was up there with the sub-lieutenant, saw what was happening and he immediately yelled to 'stand clear'. And this particular rating just didn't get, wasn't able to get out of the way in time and the sheer legs came down and hit him actually on the head and killed him instantly.[9]

Bert continued his valuable work on Tyneside while preparations for D-Day commenced. During 1943 he was posted to HMS *Volcano*, a country house in Cumbria that had been commandeered by the Navy. From there he received further practical training with explosives. This included practising the 'art' of harbour clearance at Whitehaven where 'booby traps' had to be tackled.

This was just the sort of operation that a bomb disposal officer was likely to have to mount for real in the forthcoming cross-Channel invasion.

Bert Blackmore's team during a mine/bomb-disposal operation. Note sheer legs have been rigged and set in place. (SWWEC)

However, when he finished the course rather than train for D-Day he received orders from the Admiralty to head for the Mediterranean.

In April 1944 he arrived in Egypt and rapidly expected to become involved in bomb disposal operations following landings in Greece. This was not to be and he became frustrated at kicking his heels around Cairo and Alexandria when he had his party ready for action. Eventually, his superiors were able to pacify him by ordering him to cover the coast between Alexandria and Tripoli, 'We were to clear all the mines and explosive devices that had been washed ashore. Oh it was wonderful. So . . . I chose a leading seaman to come with me who was a jolly good driver and mechanic as well as everything else. Got a five ton truck and we set off.'[10] For several weeks they drove along the North African coast blowing up various types of munitions left after the fighting in that region. In total Bert calculated they accounted for over 30 mines and explosive devices and 22 depth charges. While they might not have received much acknowledgement for this, it was still useful, potentially hazardous work.

One of their ways of tackling a mine was 'if the mine was sitting on its mechanism, mechanism plate where all the works were we would blow a little hole – hopefully – in the casing as far away from the cylinder [containing the mine's explosives] as we could and then we could place a charge on the actual case . . . And blow the lot.'[11]

When he arrived back in Alexandria Bert discovered that he had been selected for a clandestine mission in Turkey. Although Turkey was neutral, she had come under pressure to enter the war from both the Allied and Axis powers, and would eventually side with the former in the spring of 1945. He was to accompany four modern minesweepers tasked with clearing the Danube and become an adviser on the staff of the senior British Naval Officer in Turkey, Commodore D. Young-Jamieson, who was to be stationed in Istanbul.

However, owing to the speed of the Russian advance that brought them to the Danube first that plan had to be shelved. Instead, Bert had to act as an instructor on bomb and mine disposal and was briefed to 'avoid telling the Turks more than the simple "First Aid Treatment" on mines and bombs'.[12] This proved a challenge as they already knew a great deal about the subject from the Germans.

Soon the minesweepers were ordered back to the Mediterranean and Bert and another officer were tasked with coming out of Turkey overland, which included travel on an Orient Express train. Then in October 1944 Bert sailed for Greece aboard a trawler/minesweeper and took part in the landings at Piraeus (Port of Athens). These were unopposed but mines still posed a significant hazard to shipping. Once ashore Bert and his party were required to counter German attempts at demolishing the harbour's facilities:

alongside many of the quay walls the enemy sank ammunition barges and in a few instances threw large numbers of Teller mines, mortar bombs and boxes of 20mm ammunition into the water. In these cases an under water survey of the barges was carried out before they were raised and as many as possible of the Teller mines were removed so that dredging could take place.[13]

Booby traps were a further problem that they encountered and took considerable time to nullify because they often lay among important machinery or installations. Coping with the sheer quantity of munitions left by the Germans in the Piraeus area, such as a barge full of magnetic mines that had been prepared but were never laid, made for further onerous and potentially dangerous work.

While at Skaramangas naval base Bert was tasked with investigating a partially submerged German U-boat thought to be containing a new type of torpedo. It had been prepared to be destroyed as depth charges were placed alongside its hull. As it was impossible to enter it via the conning tower, access was gained by blowing a small hole near to where the torpedo racks were thought to be. In the event these proved to be empty, which must have been a severe disappointment to naval intelligence.

As the war in Europe approached its end Greece erupted into a civil war when the Communist EAM-ELAS sought to overthrow the government. As far as Bert was concerned this halted his efforts at bomb disposal and mine clearance in the country. It proved to be up to the British Army to provide troops to help support the beleaguered Greek government.

He remained ashore where, as he explained, he was able to offer assistance to the troops:

> I had a store of explosives and I couldn't just abandon them. So what I did was I took over some buildings in the old shipyard, which were ideal for what we wanted. We were able to store our explosives and all our equipment and at the same time have a room where we could sleep and stay, and this was alongside an army supply depot . . . it was handy being able to make liaison with the army and, . . . acquire some stores from them . . . in return they asked me to blow up a pillbox that was overlooking their buildings, which I did, . . . They gave me covering fire whilst I and a petty officer went along and set some explosive in and made the pillbox unusable.[14]

On leaving mainland Greece Bert was called to Crete to deal with several mines that had been discovered washed up on a beach dangerously close to the harbour. He flew down in a Wellington bomber and it was the first time that he had ever been in an aircraft. It proved to be a slightly unnerving experience:

> we were taxiing off and the rear wheel collapsed under us, so we had to get out off that and into another one . . . all good fun I suppose . . . I flew down and went on board the ship that had reported the mines, and the torpedo officer there took me out and we went and had a look at them . . . it was obvious that they had already been made safe by the Germans so all I did was I took the details of the markings and sent them in with my report, and I heard afterwards that they'd actually traced the RAF plane that had dropped them.[15]

Subsequently, Bert became involved with mine clearance around the Dodecanese, particularly on Rhodes which had been used by the Germans as a mine-laying base. Increasingly, as he was working at the tail end of the war in Europe he came across hastily assembled and unsophisticated mines consisting of 'large cartons about three foot square which were filled with explosive and the unit just placed into the centre of the explosive'.[16] To deal with these the detonators and workings of the mine were removed so that the rest could be safely dumped in the deep waters of the Aegean.

After this Greek 'odyssey' Bert was briefly posted back to Alexandria. Then in July 1945 he sailed aboard a destroyer to Ceylon (Sri Lanka) as he was destined to take part in the proposed landings in Singapore. From Ceylon he sailed to Bombay aboard a troopship *The Morton Bay*, sister ship to the famous *Jervis Bay*, and disembarked on 13 August only to find he had to await further orders.

By the time he transferred to the landing party aboard the escort carrier HMS *Activity* confusion reigned. Only later did he realise that this was owing to the two atomic bombs being dropped on Japan that had effectively ended the war. Eventually, in early September Bert did arrive in Singapore, but quickly discovered that unlike in Europe there was very little bomb disposal work to be done as the Japanese had made much less use of demolition charges than the Germans.

As he recalled, although there were a few bomb disposal tasks to be done in Singapore, none of this was especially dangerous or onerous and really the posting was 'a waste of time . . . nice as it was just sitting back and enjoying life'.[17]

Life was comfortable as the Adelphi Hotel had been commandeered by the Navy as an officer's mess. Bert and fellow officers were able to find private accommodation using their own allowances. Via official channels and an estate agent they acquired a bungalow formerly owned by a planter that came with its own band of Chinese servants, who were only too happy to work so long as they were paid in food.

Boredom began to nag away at Bert and while in the Far East he received a letter from his former employer enquiring if he was likely to be coming back to Britain. Eventually, he secured passage home aboard a cruiser and arrived during the summer of 1946. During the war he had experienced life aboard a warship as a rating and subsequently as an officer and been involved in the highly specialised, potentially hazardous and often overlooked field of bomb and mine disposal.

Bert received no specific or immediate recognition for his efforts, particularly in Greece. However, in the 1950s Bert was proud to be 'awarded' the Naval Mine and Bomb Disposal Medal, which had been specially struck for the select band of personnel who had been involved in this work.

After the war Bert married and went back to the engineering supplies firm that had employed him prior to his call-up. He worked for them for several years until being ordained in the late 1950s. Throughout his life he had a strong faith and this may well have helped him to cope with his wartime experiences. Up to his death he lived in Yorkshire and in his retirement he donated an extremely rich body of material relating to his war service to the SWWEC.

Researching the Revd C. Bert Blackmore

In April 2006 Bert was interviewed by Trevor Mumford on behalf of the SWWEC and a copy of the transcript is available in the archives there. This provides some vivid memories of his war service, particularly as a bomb and mine disposal officer in Greece during 1944–5. Additionally, SWWEC holds a fascinating selection of papers relating to Bert's war service, most of which concern wartime bomb and mine disposal. Some of these were cited above, while others such as the seventy-one-page 'Notes on Bomb Defusal and Drill' would form the basis for more detailed research into this subject.

It is worth noting that if you are interested in an individual who worked in a specialised trade such as this then they too may have kept various papers or notes that would be of value when researching their war service. Alternatively, an interesting selection of wartime training manuals/pamphlets can be found at IWM (Department of Documents) and in the library of the Royal Armouries, Leeds. The latter is open to the public Monday–Friday and for more information see: www.royalarmouries.org.

In 1994 Bert published a memoir entitled *The Explosive Years Exploits of a Royal Navy Bomb and Mine Disposal Officer, 1940–1946* (Tom Donovan Publishing Ltd), but this is an expensive book to purchase privately. More accessible books on this subject include Lieutenant Noel Cashford MBE (RNVR), *All Mine! Memoirs of a Naval Bomb and Mine Disposal Officer* (Ald Design & Print, 2002) and James Owen's *Danger UXB: The Heroic Story of the WW II Bomb Disposal Teams* (Little, Brown, 2010).

It is always worth consulting records held by TNA and while these may not have specific information on the individual or relative you wish to research, they probably will contain other material of value. Within ADM 1 Admiralty and MOD, Navy Department Correspondence and Papers are several files on mine-clearance operations. For example, ADM 1/30542 concerns the award of the French Croix de Guerre to nine members of the Navy, RNVR and Royal Canadian Naval Reserve who were stationed aboard Free French vessels. ADM 1/18387 contains documents relating to post-war mine clearance in the Mediterranean *c*. 1945–6.

Within ADM 1 material can be found relating to the hunt for the *Bismarck* and 'Force H'. Administrative records and details of training at establishments such as HMS *Collingwood* and HMS *King Alfred* may be found here too. At TNA you will also find the blue bound volumes of the *Navy Lists* near the entrance/exit to the main document reading room and these will enable you to check when an individual received his/her commission. Bruno Pappalardo's *Tracing Your Naval Ancestors* (PRO, 2003) contains further useful information, particularly on the ADM 12 indexes *c*. 1920–58.

H. T. Lenton and J. J. Colledge's *Warships of World War II* (Ian Allan Ltd, 1980) is an invaluable reference tool. Details on individual ships, such as HMS *Jersey*, can also be sought via the Internet but as always be aware that such material is unedited. Lieutenant Commander Peter Kemp's 'The Chase of the Bismarck' in *Purnell's History of the Second World War* (Phoebus Publishing Ltd, 1967), Vol. 2, No. 5, pp. 562–76 highlights the role played by 'Force H'. Two books by Brian Lavery, *Hostilities Only: Training the Wartime Royal Navy* (National Maritime Museum, 2004) and *Churchill's Navy: The Ships, Men and Organisation 1939–1945* (Conway, 2006), provide useful historical background that may be helpful when researching a relative's naval past.

Notes

1. Second World War Experience Centre, Acc. No. LEEWW 2006.199, tape 3244 transcript, Revd C. B. Blackmore interviewed by Trevor Mumford, 13 April 2006, p. 4.
2. Brian Lavery, *Hostilities Only: Training the Wartime Royal Navy* (National Maritime Museum, 2004), p. 57.
3. For more details on HMS *Jersey*, see H. T. Lenton and J. J. Colledge, *Warships of World War II* (Ian Allan Ltd, 1980), p. 110; www. uboat.net/allies/warships/ship/4452.html; and www.hmscavalier .org.uk/F72/.
4. SWWEC, Acc. No. LEEWW 2006.199, tape 3244 transcript, Revd C. B. Blackmore interviewed by Trevor Mumford, 13 April 2006, p. 7.
5. Ibid., pp. 8–9.
6. Ibid., p. 10.
7. Ibid.
8. Ibid., p. 11.
9. Ibid., p. 30.
10. Ibid., p. 15.
11. Ibid., p. 17.
12. SWWEC, Acc. No. LEEWW 2006.199, extract from paragraph 7: Directive for Lieutenant C. Blackmore (RNVR) RMS and BS Officer from Office of Flag Officer Levant and Eastern Mediterranean, 29 July 1944.
13. SWWWEC, Acc. No. LEEWW 2006.199, 'Report on the Work Carried Out By Rendering Bombs Safe Party, Piraeus Area' by Lieutenant C. B. Blackmore (RNVR) Rendering Bombs Safe Officer, Piraeus Area, p. 1.
14. SWWEC, Acc. No. LEEWW 2006.199, tape 3244 transcript, Revd C. B. Blackmore interviewed by Trevor Mumford, 13 April 2006, p. 23.
15. Ibid., p. 24.
16. Ibid.
17. Ibid., p. 28.

Chapter 5

'A Co-ed Gun Girl' at War – Ruth Aves (née Hawkins)

The Second World War was a 'people's war' in which virtually all branches of society participated in one way or another. In September 1938 with war approaching the ATS was established and at peak strength approximately 250,000 women served in it. They performed various roles notably with Anti-Aircraft Command, which operated guns and searchlights across Britain. Although an Army organization, it came under the control of RAF Fighter Command and formed a less glamorous but equally important component of the nation's air defences.

After the Blitz Lieutenant General Sir Frederick Pile C-in-C Anti-Aircraft Command came under frequent pressure to release suitable men for service elsewhere. As Churchill stated, 'it appeared indefensible to maintain 280,000 men waiting for an attack that might may never develop, if other means can be found to man the weapons'.[1] During 1941 experiments occurred with mixed anti-aircraft batteries and increasing reliance was placed upon the Home Guard and ATS to operate the guns.

By 1943 over 55,000 women were serving with Anti-Aircraft Command. Although they were not expected to heft ammunition, move guns in and out of positions or fire them, women did everything else, particularly working as fire controllers. Americans serving in Britain were reputed to be intrigued by these ATS girls. Their own armed forces didn't employ women in operational units and they referred to them as 'Co-ed Gun Girls'.[2]

Ruth Hawkins was born in January 1924 in Penang, Malaysia where her father worked in the Malayan Civil Service. However, she was sent back to Britain for her education, along with her two brothers. This was tough as they would not see their parents for four years at a stretch. Initially, none of them spoke English and relied on Malay. They were regarded as 'little urchins' by one school who refused to take responsibility 'for such unruly children'.[3]

Eventually, Ruth received some schooling in Eastbourne and Weston-super-Mare. By the early 1940s she had found employment at the Bristol Aircraft factory in Locking. Initially, the factory wanted her to measure nuts and bolts. She had little idea of what they were for but fellow workers said they were manufacturing Beaufighter aeroplanes.

Later she became an electrical inspector which was more interesting and better paid. It involved using a Lucas kit to test electrical systems before they were fitted to aircraft. Even so, the factory was noisy and the overpowering stench of aircraft 'glue' pervaded the air. Only 'Workers Playtime' on the radio served to enliven proceedings. Simultaneously, her off-duty hours were spent as an air-raid warden based at the Lamb and Flag pub in Weston.

As soon as she could Ruth applied to join the ATS. She was spurred on by the fall of Singapore and chose the Army because her father was serving in it. She did her basic training in Guildford before embarking on further instruction in Wales. Soon she experienced her first taste of military discipline. On collecting her mattress or 'biscuit' from a Nissen hut a girl with a big stripe on her arm said:

> 'What's your name?' And I thought 'oh how nice of her – Ruth "What?' she screamed at me and I said 'well you asked me my name.' 'Your surname fool.' And I said 'oh, oh, oh its, its Hawkins.' And she said 'in future you will be known as surname and number understood?' I said 'oh yes, yes I quite understand' to which she replied 'I understand corporal.'[4]

This was not perhaps the best of starts. However, Ruth tolerated the constant inspections and actually found drilling enjoyable. On passing out she was even told that she would make a good sergeant.

A further part of her training involved undertaking selection procedures for certain trades. She hoped to serve with an operational unit rather than be posted as clerk or telephonist. Ruth recalled the aptitude test:

> I put on bit of an act and I was lucky . . . we had to match up dials. We had to differentiate between aeroplanes and different things and wheels and things. Could we keep a steady hand turning a wheel? We had to have good eyesight . . . hearing . . . health and be pretty active which I was . . . and I was interested in aircraft and we were very well taught. We had to have hours and hours . . . of studying Heinkels and Stukas and Messerschmitts and, of course, our own planes because we didn't want to go knocking our own planes down . . . I really loved it.[5]

Aircraft recognition played an important part in Ruth's training and included both friendly and enemy types. Here (from left to right) can be seen the distinctive shapes of the Hawker Hurricane, Avro Lancaster and Supermarine Spitfire. (Robert Goulty)

Eventually, she was posted to 451 (M) Heavy Anti-Aircraft or 'Ack Ack' Battery from 133rd Regiment RA. The unit deployed 3.7in anti-aircraft guns. These could fire a 28lb shell 'to an effective engagement ceiling of 25,000 feet'.[6] On exploding the time-fused shells would produce hundreds of red-hot splinters that could be deadly to any aircraft within around 45ft.

Gunnery practice occurred near Whitby and Ruth was soon to have her first real taste of war. They had to fire at a 'sleeve' towed by an aircraft. A serious accident resulted when a shell exploded prematurely in the breech of one gun. It 'beheaded one of the gunners and killed one of our ATS girls, and the discipline was such that you didn't do anything other than just accept it . . . an accident . . . it was awful but you just get on with it. It's war isn't it?'[7]

For Ruth 'getting on with it' entailed working as part of a team on a predictor. This was a primitive form of computer that looked like a big box. It fed the required fire-control information to the gunners via electrical impulses down cables. By taking the height information the predictor established an aircraft's preceding flight path and estimated where it would be when shells reached it.

This data was used to calculate the correct elevation of the guns and fuse settings for the shells. Ruth remembered that typically:

the information would come perhaps from a plotting room on to our dials and we had to match the dials up to what was happening manually. And as a predictor I had to wait until my team had got the angle of the plane that was coming in, the height, the range, the speed, and I had to work out my matching up dials and what fuse I would give to get the target when we were ordered to fire. And it was pretty thrilling really, because a plane comes in at a certain angle, you go to shoot where you think it is, well I did because I didn't know. You would shoot at the plane, but of course, by the time you've shot at the plane and the shell has gone up in the air the plane has travelled so many bearings, and, of course you would miss it. So my job and my team was to find out what fuse we were going to set for the gunners to set on the shells that they would fire so far in advance of the target so that they would meet simultaneously.[8]

Enemy pilots could thwart anti-aircraft gunners by flying in a zigzag or tortuous pattern. However, this could lead to them missing their targets. The anti-aircraft guns were normally sighted so as to cover all the approaches which made it as difficult as possible for Luftwaffe bomber crews. Consequently, rather than necessarily destroying enemy aircraft an essential role of anti-aircraft guns was 'the prevention of accurate bombing'.[9] Anti-aircraft units usually operated in batteries of four guns and as the war progressed developments in gun-laying (GL) radar increased their accuracy, particularly at night.

Heavy guns, like those Ruth's battery deployed, were primarily for use against high-flying raiders (above 10,000ft). There were three main types of fire.'Continuously Pointed' fire involved each gun tracking the lead aircraft in an enemy formation. They then fired at maximum rate while it was within range or until it crossed the bomb release point. A 'Predicted Concentration', particularly useful in poor weather, entailed firing short barrages at points where it was predicted an enemy aircraft would pass. Finally, the least efficient was the 'Box Barrage' when gunners fired into a 'box' in front of what was thought to be the intended target.

By the time Ruth joined Anti-Aircraft Command in 1942 the Blitz was over but less intensive air raids still posed a threat to many British cities. Bristol, where she saw most action, continued to suffer particularly when the Luftwaffe launched retaliatory strikes in response to RAF Bomber Command operations. Operation Steinbock (Ibex) was a concerted effort in early 1944 by the Luftwaffe to target British industrial centres and ports including Bristol, for which they amassed nearly 400 bombers.

In Bristol Ruth witnessed the destruction of an enemy aircraft for the first time. She recalled 'the excitement on the command post . . . The behaviour was appalling. I shrieked louder than anybody and the smell of the cordite and the noise. It was really awful to say it but it, it really was exhilarating to see that plane come down.'[10]

Subsequently, she was demoted when an unfortunate incident occurred. Her battery had practised their drills and cut seconds off their response times when they were faced with a day-light raider. There was a new commanding officer and:

I said 'it's a Junkers Sir, it's a Junkers Sir.' And he looked at me as if I was barmy, sort of three o'clock in the afternoon. I said 'it is Sir,' and he said 'no I don't think so' . . . and we were all going like mad you see. And we had to wait for his command to engage and he didn't give it. We were on target, he didn't give that 'engage' which would mean 'fire,' you know, and he didn't. And it was a Junkers and it did come in and it did go to Filton where there was a big aircraft factory and it dropped bombs on three double decker buses killing the occupants, and for that I was posted on an aircraft recognition course. I lost my stripe, which lost my money and later I realised he was posted off and I was re-instated . . . but that was just awful and it did happen. So that was one of the saddest moments of my life.[11]

Despite incidents like the above, life on the gun lines and in camp was normally dominated by routine and discipline. This included preparing for kit inspections, writing letters and enjoying cups of tea and 'wad', or cake, at the NAAFI (Navy, Army and Air Force Institutes). Daily there would be:

all the maintenance, all that work again cleaning and scrubbing and checking batteries and one thing and another . . . Every evening we had to do lining up the guns with the instruments . . . I used to have to line them up and it would be to depress a gun to match a dial and you halted and then perhaps you had to elevate it a bit more.[12]

Sometimes during gun drills the male gunners would mess around to tease the ATS girls, especially if they knew they wanted to go off early. However, working relationships tended to be very good. The male gunners learnt to respect ATS girls especially as 'they didn't think we could do the job in the first place and they were amazed when we did, and they were very . . . congratulatory'.[13] This was reinforced by the fact that the women faced up to the same dangers as men when in action.

Morale and *esprit de corps* were key. As Anti-Aircraft Command was essentially a defensive organisation it lacked the allure of fighting formations such as Eighth Army. Even so, the girls strongly identified with the RA unit they supported. They were 'allowed to wear the grenade badge on their blouses and the AA Command formation sign on their sleeves, and the white Gunner lanyard instead of the ATS one . . . on site corporals were addressed as "bombardier" and auxiliaries as "gunner".'[14]

Ruth recalled that many of the men she was serving with were not the 'fittest . . . and were more like fathers. Some of them were sweet and I was lucky because I had a couple of them that smoked and I didn't smoke and they would say "can I have your sweet coupons?" . . . then they would say "you couldn't possibly lose some underwear could you and get some from the store because my wife is desperate for some knickers".'[15] Similarly, at some cookhouses gunners used to be able to get extra rations as their ATS and WAAF counterparts couldn't manage all their food.

Often there was time to kill. Ruth's postings to Hull and Sheffield proved far less active than Bristol. Concert parties were a good means of tackling the boredom. At Withernsea she recalled, 'I would sort of get a concert party together and everything and we would be practicing or rehearsing plays or doing something or other and I got a big show on.'[16]

Alternatively, a local Entertainments National Service Association troupe would come but they were 'so appalling that nobody would go and so it was my duty to get them into the NAAFI . . . the girls and the gunners. And when there was a good house full of people lock the doors'.[17] The troops were forced to turn it into an entertainment for themselves by seeing who could clap and cheer the lousy 'entertainers' the loudest. This helped keep everyone together.

Homesickness was another problem. Like most military units, Ruth's ATS contingents comprised people from all over the country. Mail was important and its arrival heralded a break in the monotony of the daily routine. As Ruth remembered, 'you lived for the letters'.[18] Everyone would be kind, particularly if someone had been dumped by their boyfriend or received other bad news. Similarly, 'if you felt stupid someone would talk you round and make you pull yourself together and say how lucky we were', especially when contrasted to what 'the poor civilians were going through'.[19]

Wherever they were posted discipline acted as the 'glue' bonding the unit together. This added to their shared sense of camaraderie. Anyone who was late back from visiting a boyfriend was liable to have to do punishment fatigues and be confined to barracks. When not in action or training personnel were also expected to attend 'many lectures on Army routine, Army rules, Army Hygiene'.[20]

As a civilian Ruth recalled that they had tended not to talk about the war itself even if they read about the bombing of towns and cities in the newspapers. Likewise, once in the military she discovered there was a strong emphasis on avoiding careless talk about the war. In Anti-Aircraft Command it was very much a case of getting on with the job interspersed with barrack-room routine.

Accommodation was often primitive. In Bristol they were barracked in Nissen huts and warmer but noisier wooden 'Spiders'. Typically, there were twenty to each hut with ten girls down either side. As an 18-year-old junior NCO Ruth was amazed to be in charge of an ATS section including 'much older' ladies in their late twenties. Once she had overcome her trepidation at gaining her first stripe, the power was quite enjoyable. After a year she was promoted sergeant and received her own small room with a rug. This was comparative luxury by wartime standards.

By 1944 Ruth had been transferred to 666 Heavy Anti-Aircraft (HAA) Battery RA stationed at Porton Down on Salisbury Plain. Here research into chemical warfare was conducted. This was a non-operational posting unrelated to her previous anti-aircraft work. Mainly the gunners and ATS personnel were expected to act as guards and conduct parades. While there she saw an aerial armada passing over head that heralded D-Day, the Allied Invasion of Europe, had commenced.

As the war progressed Ruth increasingly found herself holding postings that took her away from the guns. Conducting clerical work was a particular bugbear. She was offered an opportunity to train as a plotting officer underground but didn't take it as being stuck in a bunker didn't appeal to her. Instead, as a sergeant she conducted her fair share of drilling and lecturing.

Then she was made a Physical Training Instructor (PTI). It was frustrating being away from an operational unit but at least being a PTI kept her active. She was frequently involved in overseeing lengthy cross-country runs. Later, she served as a 'gas officer' responsible for providing trainees with an introduction to chemical warfare. Personnel were led through a Nissen hut full of 'gas'. Here they experienced the conditions both with and without a respirator. This taught them to recognise the feeling of being 'gassed' but it could be tough for Ruth, who often had to lead apprehensive personnel through the drill.

On VE-Day she was back at Withernsea putting on a play. The general atmosphere was euphoric but her personal celebrations were subdued. The

A wartime portrait of Ruth Aves looking very smart in her ATS service dress. Note the flaming grenade badge that ATS personnel serving with regiments of the RA were permitted to wear. (SWWEC)

war in the Far East was not over. Her father was still suffering as a POW in Japanese hands and one of her brothers had just been posted with the RAF to India. However, the mood was lifted to an extent by learning that her other brother, who was a RAF sergeant flying Lancaster bombers, had been awarded the Distinguished Flying Medal. Ruth was granted forty-eight hours' leave and together with her mother went to Buckingham Palace to watch her brother receive his decoration from King George VI.

As a tall and attractive young woman who was good at drill, Ruth was often picked out for parades with the ATS. The most notable of these was the Victory Parade in London:

> I was a marker, which means that you, keep the line straight. Whatever happens you keep your eyes to the front, and, but, of course when we got to Admiralty Arch we marched through in perfect 'V' formation, which I am very proud of, . . . And when we came to the big stand where the Queen was and King and Winston Churchill and Monty

was going past on his standing up saluting, and oh well, of course, my eyes did shift a little bit to the left but I did keep straight.[21]

After four years in the Army, Ruth was demobbed in 1946 and remained proud of her service. The Army described her 'military conduct as exemplary' and she was deemed 'efficient and trustworthy and a good leader and influence on others. Very charming and a kind disposition. Smart personal appearance.'[22] As a grandmother looking back at her wartime experience, she noted that it had taught her to value what you have in life. Her military training further highlighted the need to respect others, the importance of manners, especially punctuality, and most crucially the requirement for a good sense of humour.

Researching Ruth Aves (née Hawkins)

TNA contain various papers dealing with the ATS. Although many files date from the post-war period, within WO 32 and WO 315 can be found files dealing with issues such as the recruitment and employment of women in the Army. As so many women served alongside RA units in Britain during the war it is worth trying to find the relevant War Diary of the artillery unit concerned. Within Anti-Aircraft Command the ATS were predominantly attached to HAA units and their records can be found in WO 166 Home Forces. It helps to know the regiment concerned rather than just the battery number.

Likewise, if you wish to research someone in the ATS who was attached to an artillery unit, a visit to the Firepower Royal Artillery Museum at Woolwich could help. Be warned, they do levy a charge for private research and for more information see: www.firepower.org.uk. Notably, they hold RA War Diaries, an extensive collection of wartime pamphlets and manuals dealing with gunnery training and equipment, plus material regarding the recollections of wartime gunners.

The Woman's Royal Army Corps Museum at Guildford, which incorporated the ATS, has now closed. Its collections have been transferred to the NAM, Chelsea. A website on the ATS exists at: www.atsremembered. org.uk. As with everything on the Internet, be cautious as content is unedited. However, this site includes the personal testimony of several veterans and advice on issues such as accessing service records. At present those for the ATS are still held by the Ministry of Defence.

For Ruth Aves (née Hawkins) her interview with Mathew Smalldon on behalf of the SWWEC provided a vivid outline of her war service. Copies of the transcript of that interview are available in the SWWEC archives. If you are lucky the individual or relative you wish to research might have been interviewed by SWWEC or the IWM. Alternatively, it is worth checking whether they deposited any personal papers and/or unpublished memoirs at either of these archives.

Shelford Bidwell's *The Women's Royal Army Corps* (Leo Cooper, 1977) provides a very readable history of the ATS leading up to the formation of the WRAC in 1949. It contains a particularly helpful chapter devoted to Anti-Aircraft Command. For an accessible explanation of the technical aspects of anti-aircraft gunnery Alfred Price's *Britain's Air Defences 1939–45* (Osprey Publishing, 2004) is useful. It is lavishly illustrated which helps greatly with such a technical subject. Brigadier N. W. Routledge OBE, TD's *History of the Royal Regiment of Artillery Anti-Aircraft Artillery 1914–55* (Brassey's, 1994) is a further specialised regimental style history that covers the Second World War. Books like this are very expensive and best sought out in museums or libraries.

Another useful reference tool particularly on topics such as weapons, equipment and organisation is George Forty's *British Army Handbook 1939–1945* (Sutton Publishing, 2002). Winston Churchill took a keen interest in almost all aspects of the military throughout the war. Therefore, his six-volume history of the Second World War is worth delving into for correspondence regarding Anti-Aircraft Command. It can be obtained via libraries or second-hand book shops.

Finally, bear in mind that Anti-Aircraft Command has left its imprint on the country. Today, the remains of gun sites, like those that would have been familiar to Ruth Aves, are part of the 'archaeological heritage' of the Second World War. See: www.whateversleft.co.uk and www.urbexforums.co.uk, which both contain photographs of derelict HAA positions.

Notes

1. Prime Minister to Secretary of State for War, 10 May 1942, in Winston S. Churchill, *The Second World War Vol. IV The Hinge of Fate* (Folio Society, 2000), p. 691.
2. George Forty, *British Army Handbook 1939–1945* (Sutton Publishing, 2002), p. 319.
3. Second World War Experience Centre, Acc. No. LEEWW 2007.184, transcript of tape 3591, interview with Mrs R. Aves, née Hawkins, 7 February 2007, p. 2.
4. Ibid., p. 5.
5. Ibid., p. 6.
6. Alfred Price, *Britain's Air Defences 1939–45* (Osprey Publishing, 2004), p. 8.
7. SWWEC, Acc. No. LEEWW 2007.184, transcript of tape 3591, interview with Mrs R. Aves, née Hawkins, 7 February 2007, p. 7.
8. Ibid., p. 8.
9. Price, *Britain's Air Defences*, p. 8.

10. SWWEC, Acc. No. LEEWW 2007.184, transcript of tape 3591, interview with Mrs R. Aves, née Hawkins, 7 February 2007, p. 8.
11. Ibid.
12. Ibid., p. 21.
13. Ibid., p. 13.
14. Shelford Bidwell, *The Women's Royal Army Corps* (Leo Cooper, 1977), p. 126.
15. SWWEC, Acc. No. LEEWW 2007.184, transcript of tape 3591, interview with Mrs R. Aves, née Hawkins, 7 February 2007, p. 12.
16. Ibid., p. 10.
17. Ibid., pp. 11–12.
18. Ibid., p. 12.
19. Ibid., p. 16.
20. Ibid., p. 15.
21. Ibid., p. 22.
22. Ibid., p. 23.

Chapter Six

Flying Instructor and Bomber Pilot – Squadron Leader Denis Noel Peto-Shepherd, DFC

Denis Peto-Shepherd was born in October 1920 and attended a preparatory school in Leatherhead, Surrey. Recalling a school trip to the Hendon Air Display of 1930, he noted 'a brief appearance of the airship R101 over the airfield left me spell bound'.[1] This might have sowed the seeds of his future desire to become a pilot. However, his guardian, Admiral Kelly of Invergordon, hoped he would pursue a career in the Navy. When Denis showed no interest in the sea, he promptly packed him off to the Oratory at Caversham Park near Reading.

By 1939 Denis was enjoying the halcyon days of sixth-form life, including being a house prefect, playing 1st XV rugby and shooting with the Officer Training Corps (OTC). This was not to last, as with the German occupation of Czechoslovakia war seemed inevitable.

During the 1930s the idea of 'air fleets' being used against enemy cities gained increasing prominence, particularly under advocates of airpower such as Italian General Guilio Douhet. Denis was influenced by such thinking and when war was declared he reasoned that the greatest damage any individual could bestow upon the enemy was from the air, ideally as a bomber pilot.

After languishing in the ranks of the Local Defence Volunteers (LDV) in Surrey, where his OTC experience in handling small arms proved useful, he volunteered for the RAF. On 2 July 1940, aged 19 years and 8 months, he enlisted as 'Aircraft Hand/Aircrew' in the Royal Air Force Volunteer Reserve, the branch of the RAF that dealt with most wartime recruitment. It had been formed in 1937 to train non-commissioned pilots but in wartime its remit was extended to cover the range of aircrew plus supporting branches.

His decision to join this youthful and comparatively junior service dismayed his family. Despite the glamour associated with the aviation pioneers of the inter-war period, society still viewed the RAF with suspicion, especially when compared with the more traditional Navy and Army. Consequently, flying was deemed unsuitable employment for any kind of gentleman, not least because of the heavy technical demands it imposed on the individual.

After passing the medical and initial selection process, Denis was recommended for a commission. As an aircraftman second class he was posted to a Receiving Wing (RW) at Babbacombe near Torquay. Here men were moulded from civilians into RAF recruits. They worked a 12-hour day but there were often breaks during which they could enjoy the sunshine of the 'English Riviera'.

In November he was posted for basic training at an ITW in Newquay, Cornwall. Here pilots under training could wear the much prized white flash in their forage caps indicating they were 'Aircrew Cadets'. The course lasted six weeks and demanded strict discipline and high standards of turnout. Instruction included topics such as maths, aerial navigation, meteorology and aircraft recognition, all of which were important for potential aircrew to master. Completion of the course brought promotion to leading aircraftman (equivalent to a lance corporal), and pay increased to 5s 6d per day.

Although the recruits, or 'sprogs', had little spare time, they were also introduced to the 'delights' of the NAAFI. This stocked 'a thick and evil coloured plank'-like yellow cake known as the 'NAAFI wad', 'newspaper-flavoured grey tea or char' and 'sickly sweet and tasteless' jam tarts.[2]

In February 1941 Denis was posted to an Elementary Flying Training School at Ansty, near Coventry. Discipline was relaxed compared with basic training as the school had been a civilian establishment before being commandeered by the RAF. The aim was to have men flying as quickly as possible by completing at least 50 hours on the de Havilland D.H. 82 Tiger Moth, a two-seat biplane of inter-war design that was the standard elementary trainer.[3]

Subsequently, Denis was posted to a Service Flying Training School (SFTS) at RAF Little Rissington, Gloucestershire. Here he was free to concentrate on his flying instruction over the beautiful Cotswold countryside. However, most instructors had been NCOs in the peacetime RAF who were promoted in wartime or were survivors from the early stages of the bomber offensive. Either way, these men did not necessarily make the most effective instructors.

Teaching methods were akin to the First World War with cadets learning via copying their instructor or by trial and error when flying solo. Instruction was on the Airspeed Oxford, or 'Ox Box', a large general purpose twin-engined monoplane, that marked a significant technological step up from the Tiger Moth, not least due to its retractable undercarriage.[4] Yet its modern appearance belied some wicked characteristics, notably a tendency to spin on stalling.

Accidents were common. Denis experienced two crashes himself, one of which occurred when he attempted his first solo landing approach and hit a stone wall. This had him 'up on the carpet' before his commanding officer, but he still managed to pass basic flying training, which earned him the right to wear his 'Wings' proudly above his left breast pocket.

He re-enlisted as a pilot officer and hoped to join an Operational Training Unit (OTU) to prepare him to fly a heavy bomber. Instead, he was posted on a flying instructors' course at No. 2 Central Flying School (CFS), RAF Cranwell near Sleaford, Lincolnshire. This was the Royal Air Force College, the equivalent of Dartmouth and Sandhurst, used to train officers for permanent commissions, but in wartime its activities had been suspended.

Training continued apace using Oxfords at night and an obsolete biplane, the Avro Tutor, by day.[5] As a trainee flying instructor he became adept at using the accepted, if dated, RAF 'Patter' to demonstrate each exercise. Flying was both physically and mentally demanding, especially in the Tutor. He recalled:

> communication was by the 'Gosport' speaking tube system, which necessitated pattering into the mouthpiece against the noise of the engine, and one hand was really needed for this. Next, one's eyes were continually engaged in keeping a general look-out, and in particular scanning the ground ahead. Meanwhile a hand was required for operating the throttle through constantly varying settings.[6]

By October 1941 Denis had become a qualified flying instructor and was posted back to Gloucestershire, a county he had loved since boyhood. Here at a Flying Training School (FTS) at South Cerney he again flew the 'Ox Box'. The aim was to take pupils through the SFTS syllabus so that they progressed up to 'Wings' standard and several excitable Poles proved a challenge due to the language barrier.

Flying took place round the clock and in the vagaries of the British weather which posed a strain on all personnel. There was a constant danger that trainees might show signs of weakness, making them unsuitable as pilot material. Ideally, such individuals would be identified early and removed from flying training. Yet, throughout the war the RAF experienced around 3,000 cases per year of men succumbing to the stresses associated with flying training and most of these never flew again.

After eight months at South Cerney Denis was posted to RAF Montrose, Scotland, the new home of No. 2 CFS. Here he was to train flying instructors. It was a station of First World War vintage commanded by a veteran of that conflict who was more interested in country pursuits such as fishing than flying.

By 1940s standards it was hardly an ideal airfield being built on sand that necessitated aircraft to be fitted with desert filters. This tended to arouse excitement whenever they were away from base. Flight paths over the town and out to sea were another drawback, particularly if engine failure occurred during take-off. Flying over Scotland was also fraught with dangers owing to the unpredictable weather and mountainous topography.

Aside from the Oxford, Montrose operated the Miles Magister, an elementary trainer, and Miles Master, a single-engine advanced trainer designed to prepare fighter pilots for high-performance aircraft like the Spitfire.[7] A dash of colour and character was created by the instructors who wore privately purchased overalls on top of their RAF service dress. Denis favoured 'a black cotton overall, and with this . . . an orange scarf'.[8]

The Miles Magister entered service in the late 1930s and was the RAF's first monoplane trainer. It was used throughout the war and equipped several Elementary Flying Training Schools. (Author's photograph)

At Montrose he was promoted to acting flight lieutenant and had the satisfaction that he routinely received a favourable assessment of his flying ability. However, Denis felt that the 'real war' was passing him by so long as he was based far from the front and tied to the training machine.

Consequently, in early 1944 he was elated to receive a posting to an OTU at Wing, Buckinghamshire where he would learn to fly heavy bombers. He left Flying Training Command proud of its efforts to train desperately needed aircrew under the most trying of conditions. This work remains a less well publicised aspect of the RAF's contribution towards the Allied victory. It is sobering to note that during the war flying training accidents alone accounted for over 11,000 total casualties among aircrew.

The OTUs relieved front-line squadrons of their peacetime training role and trained aircrew in the skills and teamwork required on operations. For Denis this entailed practice as a pilot and learning how to be a bomber skipper with an appreciation of the other crew member's roles.

He trained on the Vickers Wellington in preparation for converting to heavy bombers like the Short Stirling and Avro Lancaster. Affectionately known as the 'Wimpey', the Wellington was a medium bomber of geodetic construction designed by Barnes Wallis with a six-man crew that could heft up to 6,000lb of munitions, and was armed with six to eight .303 calibre Browning machine guns.[9]

After two weeks 'crewing-up' occurred. Denis chose a bomb aimer who was 'a charming and egocentrically inclined individual who took himself and his deep interest in the arts most seriously'.[10] A tough, self-confident Australian volunteered to be his wireless operator, while as navigator he accepted a studious young man who had been reading Classics at Cambridge before joining up.

The gunners, who were to be crucial, particularly as the main form of defence on night operations, comprised a lad from Preston and a young school leaver from south Wales. Later in their training they would be joined by a flight engineer who would assist Denis in flying the aircraft.

These disparate individuals had to be moulded into an efficient fighting unit which entailed gruelling preparation on the Wellington. Day and night bombing runs and navigational skills were practised, the latter often using Gee (a radio navigation aid). Fighter affiliation exercises where the crew faced simulated attacks by RAF fighters formed another facet of their training.

Additionally, training in crash, parachute and dinghy drills was required. Having 'battled it out' successfully in the Buckinghamshire skies, the crew were posted to No. 3 Group Escape School at Methwold for an escape and evasion course.

Denis only spent a week at Methwold before being posted to a Heavy Conversion Unit at Wratting Common, Cambridgeshire. Here he flew the Stirling, the earliest of the four-engined bombers to enter RAF service. Crews had to complete 40 hours' flying on this type, which required almost continuous day and night take-offs, circuits and landings.

On 6 June 1944 he and his crew heard that the invasion of Europe (D-Day) had begun. As the subsequent struggle for Normandy developed, Denis was posted to a Lancaster Finishing School at Feltwell. Here training was designed to convert crews to that aircraft ahead of an operational posting.

He was delighted to know officially that he was definitely destined for a Lancaster-equipped squadron, and so would have a chance to pilot the kind of aircraft he had always wished to fly operationally. With the agreement of his crew he spurned the chance of promotion and a posting to the Middle East so that they could serve together in the European theatre. However, as Denis recalled, they contemplated their future with mixed feelings:

> Our excited enthusiasm in at last experiencing this outstanding aircraft was for me tempered by the realisation that, in this scheme of things, we were destined to pit ourselves against the most formidable German defences with only some twelve to fifteen hours' experience on type. This was sobering enough a thought, but with our graduation to the 'real thing' came the inevitable awareness that the existing operational loss-rate made many of our fellow course members (and for that matter ourselves) already as good as dead men.[11]

They joined No. 90 Squadron based at RAF Tuddenham, Suffolk. That squadron had flown a variety of aircraft since being re-formed in 1937. Then after an unsuccessful stint deploying some of the first American-built Boeing B-17 Flying Fortress bombers to be supplied to the RAF it was disbanded. Subsequently, the squadron was re-formed yet again so it could partake in the Combined Bomber Offensive against Germany.

By 1944 increasing resources from Bomber Command were being diverted from the strategic bombing offensive to supporting the invasion of Europe. Targets included coastal batteries, supply depots, plus the interdiction of the enemy's communications network.

On 15/16 July Denis and his crew embarked on their first sortie. They were part of a bomber force dispatched to hit the marshalling yards at Chalons-

The Avro Lancaster was a seven-seater heavy bomber, versions of which saw extensive service with the RAF during 1941–5. Arguably, it was the finest aircraft of this type produced by any of the combatant nations and the above example is preserved and flown by the Battle of Britain Memorial Flight. (Robert Goulty)

Sur-Marne, 90 miles east of Paris. Each Lancaster carried eighteen 500lb bombs. When the time on target had passed he realised they were well off course. Without a fixed reference point navigation was becoming increasingly difficult.

A single bomber away from the main stream was an easy target for predicted anti-aircraft fire and night fighters. The crew had to maintain radio silence as any transmissions could be homed in on by the enemy. This prevented them from asking for help. To make matters worse the hydraulics in the rear turret failed leaving them without their main form of defence.

Although they got the turret working using a reserve oil supply, it continued to cause problems throughout the mission. Eventually, they made a navigational fix over Paris and headed for the coast to jettison their bombs in the English Channel before flying homewards.

On their next operation to bomb marshalling yards at Aulnoye Denis and his crew became lost again. Back at base they realised that their motivation was becoming suspect and their navigator was sent away for re-training. His replacement came from a crew that had been broken up and Denis feared the new man would damage his crew's morale as he appeared gripped by fear. Fortunately, they were later rejoined by their original navigator who proved successful.

As Denis's tour progressed he was tasked with raids on industrial targets in the Rhur, known as 'Happy Valley' by RAF aircrews, which entailed his squadron reverting to the strategic bombing role. His crew was able to rely on 'Fishpond', a fighter detection device linked to their onboard H2S radar navigational equipment. Together these technical innovations enabled crews to adopt practicable tactics.

Denis discovered that flying just above the main bomber stream had several advantages, especially as the position of his aircraft relative to that stream could be checked by using 'Fishpond'. Although unwise for a bomber to be caught alone, 'Fishpond' enabled the wireless operator and bomb aimer to warn of approaching enemy fighters before they were in visual range. Similarly, the wireless operator would listen out for combats and report on these before any contact occurred.

Raids on Germany were fraught with dangers for aircrew, not least of which were the sophisticated anti-aircraft defences of the Kammhuber Line, named after the German general responsible for implementing them. By 1944 devices like Gee could help overcome these to an extent by allowing bombers to swamp defences en mass. However, throughout the campaign the Germans adapted and modified their defences so that searchlights, concentrated anti-aircraft fire and night-fighters were a perpetual threat to Allied bombers.

Defences included Wurzburg radar units that directed night-fighters to intercept bombers. As they approached a target bombers also risked being caught by radar-controlled searchlights. These were often deployed alongside ones that were manually operated so that seventy to eighty searchlights might probe the sky simultaneously. Additionally, the Germans were skilled at deploying weather conditions to their advantage. By shinning searchlights onto clouds below bombers, 'Mattscheibe', or 'ground glass', was created, an opaque screen against which they were easily visible to night-fighters.

Often night-fighters would harass returning bombers all the way to the Dutch coast, a distinctly unnerving experience especially when the ground was littered with the flaming wrecks of those that had been caught. Unsurprisingly, after raids deep into enemy territory Denis and his crew were always particularly relieved to return to Tuddenham where mugs of hot coffee laced with rum would be pressed into their hands by awaiting WAAF personnel.

On 23 July 1944 Denis and his crew were part of a 600-strong force sent to bomb Kiel. They did so in the knowledge that an attempt had been made on Hitler's life. Part of their bomb load included propaganda leaflets exhorting German workers to follow the lead of their generals who had called for a swift end to the war.

The bombers were to fly over the North Sea below 2,000ft (at 300ft if possible) to avoid radar detection and pass through a Mandrel screen. This was an airborne system of radio counter-measures carried by other aircraft used to jam the German Freya early warning radar. Once through the screen the bombers would rise to 20,000ft and drop 'Window', strips of metal designed to confuse enemy radar by overloading their system with contacts.

These counter-measures proved successful and they reached Kiel intact. However, over the target Denis was puzzled by several loud explosions. He thought this might have been naval gunfire from the base below but later it transpired these were in fact other bombers being blown to pieces by direct hits from anti-aircraft shells.

Danger not only came from the enemy as crews also ran the risk of mechanical failures and accidents, serious concerns when dealing with a bomber loaded with fuel and munitions. At the end of July Denis took off on a deep-penetration raid against Stuttgart. This called for all his skill as a pilot when his Lancaster suffered problems, rendering it unable to take part in the sortie. On only three engines and with his aircraft awash with fuel from a leak, he managed to land safely at Tuddenham, after having jettisoned his bomb load over the Wash.

As the war progressed No. 90 Squadron were tasked with hitting tactical targets in support of ground forces and V weapons sites in France. Although flying time was much shorter for these operations than raids into Germany, the dangers were equally as great. In daylight the heavily laden, low-flying bombers were prime targets for Luftwaffe fighters and light anti-aircraft guns.

After a heavy bombing raid on Caen Denis recalled that on landing 'we were left with our teeth still rattling inside our heads'.[12] Operations against German units trapped in the Falaise pocket were particularly disturbing. Cloud obscured the target and Denis was aware that several bombers flew above it and dropped their munitions oblivious of whether they hit friend or foe.

Tension, fatigue and fear were an omnipresent part of life for all bomber crews. Before each operation there was a briefing with a raft of detail from specialist officers, which could heighten the level of stress surrounding an impending mission. Every occasion a crew was on the 'Battle Order' for a

An extract from one of Denis's 'RAF Flying Log Books' showing his final missions flown with 90 Squadron during October–November 1944. Documents like this are the sort item that may survive within families and can be used to trace the wartime career of a relative. (SWWEC)

mission the strain only really lifted once that operation was completed. Even then this was tempered by the knowledge that the whole process would soon start all over again.

Crews tended to develop a fatalistic attitude and as Denis explained, 'you either bought it or you did not'.[13] Consequently, life at base tended to feel transient too, especially as losses were frequently high. Many crews developed rituals intended to bring luck and ensure their safe return, such as kissing the scarf a girlfriend had given them or urinating on the tail wheel of a bomber. Reflecting on this after the war Denis was moved to write:

> my own experience would not allow me to say there was no such thing as chance, or good fortune; in operational flying the survival of a crew was chiefly dependent upon unity of purpose, discipline, professional competence, close co-operation, concern and interest for

each other and sustained determination to destroy the enemy. These breed confidence, the success of which should never be confused with luck.[14]

The approach to a target was particularly daunting for bomber crews. Describing a raid on Bremen on 18/19 August 1944 Denis stated:

From a distance this glowing, pulsating mass seemed to be throwing high into the sky above it, a huge canopy of twinkling sparks and cascading colours. It was tempting to dismiss it all as some gigantic, light hearted and inconsequential fireworks display, and to evade the reality that it was a stricken city blazing amidst clouds of bursting shells, falling target markers and hundreds of tons of bombs shrieking into the billowing smoke of a dreadful destruction.[15]

The implications of such raids concerned Denis during the war. Notably, he recalled that it was perturbing, when tasked with dropping incendiaries on Brunswick, to be told at the briefing that 'the workers houses will burn well'.[16]

In September 1944 he was promoted acting squadron leader in command of 'A' Flight No. 90 Squadron. He was involved in daylight as well as night deep-penetration raids on enemy cities as the tide of war flowed against Germany. By now he had gained considerable combat flying experience and practice in delivering conventional high-explosive bombs plus incendiaries. With his crew he also became adept at mine laying, known by the RAF as 'gardening', a task that could be done highly accurately using H2S radar.

Additionally, Denis's operational experience encompassed both strategic and tactical bombing. The latter notably included raids on Le Havre, which assisted in forcing the German garrison to surrender. However, his most unusual sortie was in support of the hard-pressed airborne forces at Arnhem on 22 September.

As part of 'Operation Special' No. 90 Squadron was tasked with dropping dummy paratroopers to act as a diversion. These were small hessian figures complete with helmets and parachutes that looked realistic from distance. To add to the illusion they were fitted with flares and cartridges that would imitate small arms fire. Unfortunately, the ploy failed to deceive the Germans.

His final operation occurred on 11 November and was a daylight attack against an oil refinery at Castrop-Rauxel in the Rhur. Reflecting on his tour with Bomber Command Denis noted that by the end of it he and his crew, 'were a group of men united by one of the strongest bonds known to mankind, that of men who put to the supreme test in action stood steadfastly together. Such a knowledge of ones fellows is a precious thing which is almost impossible to come by outside the intense experiences of war.'[17] He had undertaken thirty-three sorties, many of them in his favourite Lancaster Mk III 'R' for Roger Number PB204, and despite his inauspicious start had become an able bomber skipper and flight leader. He was awarded the Distinguished Flying Cross for his service with Bomber Command and his recommendation commented:

> This officer has set a fine example by his cool and unassuming leadership and high standard of pilotage. He has never failed to make the most earnest endeavours to carry out his attacks with determination and accuracy, and the results achieved have been most satisfactory . . . By his own zeal and industry, he has moulded his crew into a highly efficient unit. Latterly, when he assumed command of an operational flight, he has willingly and quietly taken great pains to improve the general organisation of his flight, and has engendered in it a most excellent team spirit.[18]

Subsequently, Denis hoped to serve with Tiger Force in the strategic bombing of Japan, especially as he wanted to join his brothers serving in that theatre. However, given his flying experience he was offered a second tour over Europe with Bomber Command as a Pathfinder (a skilled pilot deployed to mark targets for bombers). He declined and was assigned flying training duties for the remainder of the war.

Initially, he worked as an instructor at No. 12 OTU at Chipping Warden, near Banbury and was then posted to No. 17 OTU at Turweston. He spent both VE-Day and VJ-Day quietly going about base routines. In particular, these postings entailed dealing with problems of ill discipline and flying accidents, a subject with which Denis was all too familiar after his previous experience gained with Flying Training Command.

It was long, arduous work as the RAF was starting to gear up for its post-war role and many airmen were effectively 'demob happy'. In contrast to the high octane life of a bomber skipper it must have been a disappointment, especially as he had hoped to experience active service in the Far East.

After the war Denis opted to stay in the RAF and in 1947 was among the first officers to be granted a permanent commission. He retired in 1963 with the rank of squadron leader having completed numerous postings, married and had a family. One of his most interesting post-war appointments was as the aide-de-camp to the British Ambassador in Bagdad, Iraq (1948–50).

Researching Denis Noel Peto-Shepherd

More details of Denis's war service can be gleaned from his riveting memoir, *The Devil Take the Hindmost* (Pentland Press, 1996), which vividly describes his childhood, school days and RAF career before he joined No. 90 Squadron. His unpublished memoir covers his operational tour with Bomber Command and post-war service, a copy of which can be found in the archives of the SWWEC.

Additionally, SWWEC hold Denis's Form 414 RAF Pilot's Flying Log Books, *c.* 1940–58. These recorded all his flights as a wartime trainee, flying instructor, bomber skipper and in the post-war RAF. Ideally, when researching a pilot it is extremely useful to have access to such material. A further source of Flying Log Books is AIR 4 at TNA. Alternatively, if the individual you wish to research is still alive you might like to ask them if they kept any such documents and would be happy for you to view them. Many pilots kept their log books and it is also worth checking whether they passed them on to members of their family.

The SWWEC possess several of Denis's wartime notebooks detailing information on subjects such as meteorology that were important for pilots to appreciate. Extracts from these plus items of his wartime uniform can be viewed on the SWWEC website at: www.war-experience.org/collections/air/alliedbrit/ peto-shepherd.

Denis's wartime career can be neatly followed via official documents at TNA. While these provide scant personal details about him, they do put his wartime experiences into an operational context, particularly his tour with No. 90 Squadron. AIR 32 Training Command contains a report on the history and organisation of flying training *c.* 1914–45. Records for the training organisations to which Denis was posted, further details of which can be found in his memoirs, are in AIR 29 Miscellaneous Units.

ORBs for No. 3 Bomber Group and No. 90 Squadron covering January–December 1944 are in AIR 25 and AIR 27 respectively. AIR 28 Stations contains ORBs for RAF Tuddenham which supplements the information found in his memoirs. AIR 50 comprises Combat Reports including those for No. 90 Squadron spanning August 1941–August 1944.

Finding Denis's recommendation for the DFC posed a significant challenge and I am extremely grateful to Mr Paul Baille for supplying a facsimile. He has compiled a private index of the award files held within AIR 2 at TNA. For further information please contact: Mr P. Baille, 14 Wheatfields, St Ives, Huntingdon, Cambridgeshire PE17 6YD, email: paulbaillie@tiscali.co.uk.

David Mondey's *The Hamlyn Concise Guide to British Aircraft of World War II* (Chancellor Press, 1995) is an invaluable reference tool detailing all types of aircraft of British manufacture employed by the wartime RAF. John Buckley's *Air Power in the Age of Total War* (UCL Press, 1999) discusses the doctrine and theory of air power with reference to strategic bombing. While reprints of Giulio Douhet's *The Command of the Air* are available, including one published by the Office of Air Force History, Washington DC, 1983.

There are numerous works detailing the activities of Bomber Command and the following are intended as a guide for those wishing to conduct their own research: Max Hastings's *Bomber Command* (Pan Books, 1999) and John Terraine's *The Right of the Line* (Wordsworth Editions Ltd, 1998) discuss the strategic bombing offensive from its inception to the eventual defeat of the Luftwaffe and fall of Nazi Germany.

Over 50,000 British and Commonwealth aircrew perished in the pursuit of this offensive. Richard Overy's *Why the Allies Won* (Pimlico, 1995) contains a stimulating chapter entitled 'The Means to Victory: Bombers and Bombing' as part of his analysis into the reasons for the Allied victory in 1945.

By contrast, Patrick Bishop's *Bomber Boys Fighting Back 1940–1945* (Harper Perennial, 2008) is an account compiled from the perspective of individuals who served in Bomber Command. It relies heavily on the personal testimony of veterans. Similarly, Stephen Darlow's *D-Day Bombers the Veteran's Story: RAF Bomber Command and the US Eighth Air Force Support to the Normandy Invasion 1944* (Grub Street, 2004) includes personal testimony from former aircrew, including a member of No. 90 Squadron.

The following general histories contain sections on Bomber Command: Christopher Chant's *The History of the RAF: From 1939 to the Present* (Regency House Publishing Ltd, 1993); Chaz Bowyer's *The Royal Air Force 1939–1945* (Pen & Sword, 1996); and Air Chief Marshal Sir Michael Armitage's *The Royal Air Force: An Illustrated History* (Brockhampton Press, 1998).

Useful websites include: www.wartimememories.co.uk/airfields/ tuddenham. html, which contains personal recollections of life at that station; www.rafmod .uk/bombercommand/h90.html and www.historyofwar.org/air/units/RAF/90 outline the service history of No. 90 Squadron. These can also be used to search for other wartime RAF squadrons.

Notes

1. Denis Peto-Shepherd, *The Devil Take the Hindmost* (Pentland Press, 1996), p. 9.
2. Ibid., p. 100.
3. Details of the Tiger Moth can be found in David Mondey's *The Hamlyn Concise Guide to British Aircraft of World War II* (Chancellor Press, 1995), pp. 72–3.
4. Ibid., pp. 10–11 (contains details on the history and development of the Airspeed Oxford).

5. Ibid., p. 22 (contains details on the history and development of the Avro Tutor).
6. Peto-Shepherd, *The Devil Take the Hindmost*, p. 149.
7. Details of the Miles Magister and Miles Master can be found in Mondey's *The Hamlyn Concise Guide to British Aircraft*, pp. 168–9, 176–7.
8. Peto-Shepherd, *The Devil Take the Hindmost*, p. 211.
9. Further details on the Wellington, Stirling and Lancaster can be found in Mondey's *The Hamlyn Concise Guide to British Aircraft*, pp. 217–21, 189–92, 28–32 respectively.
10. Peto-Shepherd, *The Devil Take the Hindmost*, p. 253.
11. Ibid., p. 275.
12. Second World War Experience Centre, Acc. No. 2000.456 (Box 1 of 5), Denis Noel Peto-Shepherd Papers, unpublished memoir, p. 531.
13. Ibid., p. 550.
14. Ibid., p. 567.
15. Ibid., pp. 553–4.
16. Ibid., p. 539.
17. Ibid., p. 622.
18. TNA, AIR 2-8829 Master File, Folder Air 2-8830, No. 73 Recommendations for Honours and Awards: Fl/Lt. (Acting Sqn Ldr) 102303 Denis Noel Shepherd, Award of DFC 29 November 1944.

Chapter 7

An Infantryman on the Italian Front –
Bill Titchmarsh

During the Second World War the Army 'absorbed nearly three million men, three-quarters of whom were conscripts'.[1] These men came from a variety of backgrounds and had to be moulded into effective soldiers. Bill Titchmarsh was one of those who experienced life at the sharp end as an infantryman, particularly at Anzio which he later described as a 'slaughterhouse'.[2]

Bill was born in August 1921 and was one of seven children whose father was often away at sea. Educated at the Royal Merchant Navy School Bearwood, Berkshire, he was destined to follow suit but seasickness prevented this. In the early 1940s he lived with his family in Southampton and worked as a 'cardex clerk' at the Supermarine Spitfire works at Woolston, 'during the day all the tools required were put on a chit and signed by the foreman and passed to me and I would write it on the card index system and then the supervisor used to check them and do the ordering'.[3]

Soon he experienced the war at first hand as Southampton's aircraft industry became a target for the Luftwaffe. He had joined the LDV as a messenger boy equipped with a bicycle and rifle but no ammunition. During one air raid the string holding his rifle to the bicycle snapped and went through the spokes sending him flying. He was very lucky. The next bomb fell 150yd away and the blast would probably have killed him had he still been upright.

At Woolston there was a sandbag emplacement with a Lewis gun. Bill used to be allowed to sit there provided he told the LDV Sergeant in a nearby pub if there was any trouble.

One night a Jerry plane came down river . . . gliding about 500ft, engines cut out and I could see the people in the plane but I didn't know how to fire the gun. I could have shot it down like that! I followed it all the way round . . . I dashed in and told the men but they didn't believe me of course.[4]

Bill witnessed the effects of the bombing on his local community. He had to help a friend's father, who suffered from crippling rheumatoid arthritis, into their air-raid shelter. While 200yd from his house a school suffered a direct hit.

Owing to the bombing aircraft production was dispersed. Subsequently, Bill was sent to a factory at Trowbridge, Wiltshire. He didn't enjoy it. When his call-up papers arrived instead of handing them in to be marked as a reserved occupation he posted them back. A fortnight later he received an envelope containing a rail ticket and a 1s postal order for lunch.

The train from Southampton stopped near Weymouth owing to a landslide. Everyone had to walk to the station. With around twenty other men, Bill was met by soldiers who herded them onto trucks destined for Bodmin. Here they were to do their basic training with the Duke of Cornwall's Light Infantry.

After a few days Bill was promoted squad leader and summoned to a meeting about the mess. This gave him an early insight into the military mindset. He had received a complaint from other recruits about dirty mugs:

> there was a queue of about 250 people in two lines in front of the double doors waiting to go into the mess. A sergeant came out and said 'Anybody here by the name of Titchmarsh?' Bill said 'Yes sergeant.' The sergeant replied 'Ah come with me . . . lift up that mug is that alright?' 'Well it is a bit dirty Sergeant.' 'Right you can come back here at 2 pm and clean the Bloody lot!'[5]

After that Bill wasn't so keen to remain squad leader but was told to persevere. The recruits did drill, cross-country running, marches and went on the firing range. Bill enjoyed it and proved a good shot. Additionally, there were lectures organised by the Army Bureau of Current Affairs, intended to promote discussion of topical events.

From Bodmin Bill was drafted into the Royal Militia Isle of Jersey (RMIJ). In 1940, with the threat of German occupation imminent, the single battalion RMIJ received permission to serve outside Jersey. Consequently, it was re-formed as 11th (RMIJ) Battalion the Hampshire Regiment. It remained stationed in Britain but supplied several drafts for overseas.

When Bill joined the RMIJ in 1943 they were based at Withernsea on Humber and later served in County Durham. On arrival he didn't know where to go as there were no signs. He was told:

A wartime photograph of a youthful Private No. 14396143 Titchmarsh while stationed in Britain.
(Author's collection)

see that light house the army is over there. It was dark and I followed
a soldier into a building and managed to grab a spare bed. Next day I
reported to the office handed them my envelope. The Quarter Master
Sergeant looked after me. I didn't do anything for a couple of days just
turned up for meals followed the boys then we had a parade. What a
slovenly bunch we were as we had all come from different units and
had to be put through our paces now we'd joined the 'real army'.[6]

Bill was good at drill and picked to do a guard duty one night. He was told
to challenge everyone that came down the road:

About 11 pm I heard loud chatter and jollifications coming down the
avenue, dark it was, so I stepped out 'Halt' and clicked the bolt on my
rifle. 'Don't shoot, don't shoot' came the reply. So I said 'Come forward
and be recognised' and I clicked the bolt again even though I had no
ammunition.[7]

It was the commanding officer, second in command and regimental sergeant major (RSM). Next morning he was summoned, praised for his alertness and promoted lance corporal. However, if posted on active service Bill would have to revert back to the rank of private.

Afterwards he was regularly chosen to conduct demonstrations for the other troops. Once he had to jump off a small cliff onto a sandy beach. Unfortunately, on landing he hit a stone and the impact ruptured his Achilles tendon. This forced him to spend three weeks on crutches while working in the company offices.

On recovering Bill was dispatched to a War Office Selection Board at Catterick. These were instituted during 1942 and used to pick potential candidates for officer training. They deployed psychologists and psychiatrists and part of their remit was to eradicate the idea that only the privileged could obtain commissions.

The pace was hectic. Frequently there were night exercises followed by morning lectures. Candidates arrived back at barracks exhausted. Bill fell asleep during one lecture and was rounded on by the instructors. He was hauled before the brigadier who said, 'Ah, the man who can't keep his eyes open. Well you're no good to us here if you can't keep awake.'[8] Bill tried to explain that he had been on exercise for two consecutive nights. It was to no avail. Soon he was attached to 9th Battalion Royal West Kent Regiment based at Blackburn. They operated solely as a training unit. Life was dominated by drill, weapons training and exercises. Once he witnessed a Guards instructor demonstrate 'How not to cock the PIAT' (Projector Infantry Anti-Tank) using a dummy round. The weapon 'went off' and later the instructor died of internal injuries.

Life was made particularly unpleasant by the platoon sergeant major who put Bill on charges for trivial offences. In every draft the platoon sergeant major picked on an individual and unfortunately this time it was Bill's turn. Frustrated by this treatment, he saw the RSM who told him to 'stick it out'. Increasingly fed up with soldiering at home, Bill applied for an overseas draft.

Three weeks later he was heading for a reinforcement camp in North Africa where he stayed for several weeks prior to being shipped to Italy. Logically, as Bill was from the RMIJ, he would have joined a battalion from the Hampshire Regiment. However, casualties were such that he was drafted into 2/6th Queen's Royal Regiment (West Surrey), a Territorial battalion in 169th Queen's Brigade. They were part of 56th London Division, a formation that eventually experienced extensive service in Italy.

When Bill joined 2/6th Queens they were recovering from operations on the Cassino Front. As their war diarist explained, conditions were:

> exhausting, especially for rifle companies with very cold weather . . . latterly very wet they have had no cover from the elements and at least two platoons were unable to move in daylight owing to enemy snipers. Silent patrols have been almost impossible owing to rocky terrain, hence the difficulty in obtaining the ever needed prisoners. Limited supplies all had to be brought up by porters.[9]

The Germans had withdrawn to the Gustav Line which ran from the mouth of the Garigliano to the Adriatic. Operations were bogged down in a bloody stalemate made all the worse by the winter conditions and rugged topography that were a great hindrance, particularly to attacking forces.

Operation Shingle, an amphibious assault at Anzio, was an attempt by the Allies to bypass the enemy lines and hasten their progress up the Italian peninsula. It was to be launched by VI Corps, in conjunction with a thrust by 5th Army south of Cassino, and scheduled for 22 January 1944.

The commander of VI Corps, American Major General J. P. Lucas, stuck to the letter of his orders and secured the beach-head rather than advancing inland, believing this would draw German units away from Cassino. Controversy has raged over his decision ever since. For their part the Germans hastily rushed reinforcements to Anzio and by the end of January they had contained the Allied threat.

Bitter fighting ensued throughout the following months until in May VI Corps broke out and met 5th Army which was advancing after the fall of Cassino. The 'Allies lost 7,000 killed and 36,000 wounded or missing . . . and a further 44,000 non-battle casualties who were hospitalised due to injuries and sickness'.[10]

During 17–18 February 169th Brigade assembled in Naples ahead of sailing to Anzio. As part of 56th Division they were being pulled out from the Cassino Front and deployed as urgently required reinforcements in the beach-head.

En route the Arethusa class cruiser HMS *Penelope,* nicknamed 'HMS Pepperpot' by the troops, was torpedoed by the German submarine U-410. She had been travelling at speed making an awkward target for the U-boat, but once hit she sank within minutes. This was very unnerving for Bill and the other troops who witnessed it.

On landing at Anzio 'the place was as quiet as a kitten so we marched in about a mile, sat down and brewed up'.[11] Soon the men gained an impression of the type of country they would have to fight over. It was significantly different from the mountainous terrain further south, 'flat, thinly cultivated, with few roads, the woods low and sparse and the farms poor and scattered. Many wadis wound through and gave the only cover from the enemy observation from the Alban Hills; otherwise every single object on the beach-head was in full view'.[12] This terrain on the left of the beach-head 'favoured fighting of an intermingled and confused kind'.[13] Soon Bill experienced this as a member of 14 Platoon 'C' or 'Charlie' Company 2/6th Queens:

> you didn't know who was on the right of you or left. You knew who was in front sometimes. We had to do a force march as the Cheshires [the divisional machine-gun battalion] had been cut off. This sergeant took us in at the double. We just had our rifles and spare ammunition bandoliers but they got themselves out of trouble when we arrived.[14]

Both sides engaged in savage raids, attacks and counter-attacks throughout February and March. Bill's battalion was frequently deployed to plug any gaps. As he observed, 'we came out of the line, used to rest sometimes only for a few hours, then we had to get back in as best we could'.[15]

Artillery and naval gunfire was crucial. During February–March the field regiment supporting 169th Brigade 'fired 54,000 rounds in a fortnight'.[16] Bill remembered:

> it was the guns that saved Anzio . . . the gunners were firing hub to hub . . . right over your head and sometimes on us. Once we called a 'stonk' down on us and were told to get down in the bottom of our slit trenches with Jerry all around. Luckily the rounds fell on open ground amongst the enemy and not in the slit trenches.[17]

Frequently Bill manned a listening post in an advanced position. On one occasion he was, 'told to fire on sound as there were no patrols in our area whatsoever. At 1am there was a hell of a noise. I fired a whole magazine of my Bren gun and changed it. Someone said "Stop firing! Cease fire. Patrol coming in." I was upset about that.'[18] Fortunately, nobody was killed, although one bullet did nick a British soldier on the nose.

In the listening post Bill was accompanied by his mate Willy. Although no soldier, Willy wasn't a coward either. He had been a music teacher in peacetime and was in his mid-thirties, an old man compared to the rest of 14 Platoon. He was always slow and had a severe squint that was mistaken as a mark of insubordination by officers and NCOs. Bill was told to look after him.

After one engagement the order came to 'make your own way back as best you can'. Bill said:

'come on Willy pick up that other Bren and lets go'. He had his boots in his hand and we got into a wadi full of water. Jerry bullets were flying around our heels. Anyway we got into this wadi and I fired my Bren at three or four of them about 50–60 yards away. I saw them go down but don't know if I killed them. Then we moved into another bloody wadi, a big deep ravine like a lobster claw full of brown dirty water. Jerry flung grenades into the one we had just vacated. And we waited for half an hour there and heard them go away.

After half an hour we decided we could make it. I got on the escarpment and was so disorientated I didn't know which way to go. Willy said 'Don't ask me I don't know which way to bloody well go! ' We sat there for about twenty minutes and all this shit was flying around. Suddenly our guns opened up . . . Jerry put a big attack in. We knew which way to go then [by following the sound of their own artillery] . . . and found our company commander.[19]

Later they formed up for a counter-attack when the hapless Willy was tragically wounded by friendly fire. The infantry were to advance 15 minutes behind the barrage but first had to negotiate an awkward irrigation ditch. Unfortunately, several shells fell among the British troops. An officer courageously ran out and tried to signal the guns to stop with his flare pistol. The man on Bill's right was killed and amid the chaos he lost track of Willy. Bill helped tend to some of the wounded:

we tried to carry this fellow and he had a hole the size of a tea cup in his back. He fell off the stretcher that's how I noticed it. We got him back . . . and rushed to . . . the doctor . . . a Herculean effort it was. The doctor came up to me 'Get him out!' 'He is still alive Sir.' 'Well take him outside and let him rest.' So I took him out and he died.[20]

It was then Bill noticed another soldier 'completely covered in bandages, except for over one eye . . . I recognised Willy – he was squinting!'[21]

After the war he was able to get in touch with Willy and arrange a visit. Bill was in for a shock. Willy was in a harness with, 'his right leg off below the knee, the other one above the knee, and his left arm off at the shoulder. I couldn't believe it. I stayed with him about 30 minutes and his wife comes up and says "You will have to go . . . the nurses are coming to dress him".'[22] Willy's wife asked Bill not to visit again. Although he was mortified, he could understand her bitterness, particularly towards the Army. To this day Willy is often in his thoughts.

After 'their hard tour of duty in the Anzio beach-head' 169th Brigade were due to re-fit in the Middle East.[23] However, on the eve of their departure 2/6th Queens were attached to Force 266 assisting Yugoslav partisans fighting the Germans. Bill remembered that these were a fearsome crowd. His battalion's war diarist agreed, 'women march with the men carrying a pack bigger than our webbing valise, and full of equipment. Hand grenades at their belts, and a rifle or machine gun over their shoulder.'[24] The battalion did not see combat but fulfilled logistical tasks, including providing work parties to clear a landing strip on the island of Vis.

After Yugoslavia the battalion was stationed briefly in Egypt in preparation for deployment to the Middle East, but in fact they were to be posted back to Italy. Training included 'infantry and tank co-operation, a battalion in night attack exercise and company test schemes'.[25] Bill was a candidate for promotion to sergeant, but he was relieved when this went to someone else, as virtually all NCOs and platoon officers had become casualties. While there the battalion was pleased to hear that Rome had fallen; the men felt proud that they had contributed to this victory.

By late July 1944 the battalion was in Italy again. If the Gothic Line was breached it appeared they might be deployed in a 'pursuit battle'.[26] This line was a series of German defensive positions stretching south of Bologna roughly via Pisa and Florence to Ancona. However, at Taranto Bill contracted malaria despite having 'turned himself yellow with Mepacrine'.[27] He had a severe headache, was partially blinded, but was somehow dragged along by his mates as they marched.

Soon he was hospitalised and then posted to a reinforcement camp. He was desperate to get back to his unit rather than risk being drafted elsewhere. On discharge from the hospital he recalled, 'I had lost a lot of weight through sweat … there was a heap of coats, gas masks and rifles. I was sent to pick this coat up … a Guardsman's coat came down to the floor, long sleeves and I held onto it'.[28] This would later serve him well on sentry duties during the Italian winter of 1944–5. Fortunately, at the reinforcement camp Bill spotted a truck emblazoned with the 'Black Cat' badge of 56th Division and hitched a lift northwards.

En route he slept in a house with other soldiers. That night the Luftwaffe bombed it killing several men and leaving Bill dazed. 'I was badly bruised and lost my hearing and couldn't taste or smell anything.'[29] He ended up back in the same hospital he had only recently vacated.

Eventually, Bill did manage to get back to 2/6th Queens. In mid-September they were involved in heavy fighting at Monte Croce. Bill remembered coming under artillery fire during an assault, 'I always took my pack off put it over my head when we got down [under fire] like that . . . If he got up [the man in front] I got up and if he didn't get up I wouldn't get up.'[30] Suddenly an officer came running up to Bill and said, 'get up!'. The man in front had been killed and the rest of the unit was 200yd ahead, having been held up by the enemy. Eventually, the troops doubled up onto a plateau where there were haystacks that provided a limited form of cover.

Fearful that tracer fire might set the hay alight, they moved on. The platoon expected a swift counter-attack, as the Germans were adept at these, but it failed to materialise. Instead, from out of the bushes Bill, 'saw this woman and she was dragging some crutches. I said "don't fire. There's an old woman down there coming up. Look to your front!".'[31] The woman appeared with two crutches and was coming up the hillside on her elbows. Bill went forward, picked her up and was nearly strangled by her as she grabbed hold of the rabbit's foot he wore around his neck. Bill's mother had given him this as a lucky charm and he obeyed her instructions to never take it off, 'you can imagine the stick I got in the showers. But I was in so many scrapes where people were killed next to me and I was unscathed.'[32]

By now the Italian campaign had become a strategic backwater. Since D-Day the Allies had firmly focused their attentions on North-West Europe. However, it was imperative that units in Italy, including 2/6th Queens, pinned down as many German troops as possible so as to ease pressure elsewhere. Infantry were becoming short of manpower and increasingly personnel were drafted from other arms, particularly the Royal Artillery.

Throughout the winter of 1944–5 Bill was involved in tough fighting, notably around Faenza and at the River Senio as part of operations that would contribute towards the eventual surrender of German forces in Italy. He recalled one action where:

> My section were sent to the right and luckily there was a sunken road there and soldiers from 'B' Company were lying dead on the ground. We picked up their dog tags and continued up the side of the church. There was an avenue of Poplar trees . . . and 20 yards away a sunken well . . . we got in there. This Jerry comes out for a pee . . . we fired above him and rushed after him. There were these half tracks laden ready to go, it was a HQ unit, and I threw a grenade but it didn't go off [it had not been primed].
>
> I shouted in German 'come out' and there were majors, captains and a colonel. Very rare to capture them. We sent them back and they

were being shot at [by their own men in the church tower]. So we put a few shots up and they came down. I told the doctor about the medical supplies in the half track and he comes up in his jeep.[33]

Bill had to escort the colonel back to battalion HQ. It was pouring with rain and he prodded him along with his bayonet. On witnessing this, his CO gave the German a kick and forced him to hand over his gas cape so Bill could keep dry.

Later at the Senio Bill's battalion had to clear the river bank of Germans:

We were in these Buffaloes [tracked armoured amphibious load carriers] and it was arranged by partisans . . . for people in houses to put sheets out to signal that there were no Germans . . . there was this little wooden bridge and the driver decided it wouldn't hold the weight of his Buffalo. He was ordered to and went backwards to get a good run up. Jerry comes out with their hands up. About 50–60 of them and we sent them back and continued the hunt.

. . . there was this house and the white sheet had not completely come down so I tapped the driver and said 'We will check this one.' We went in and it was full of Italians very friendly, no Jerries, and they gave us this wine . . . coor that warmed us up. I staggered out and I couldn't get inside this 'tank'. The CO comes up and says 'What have you got there?' 'Something for the officers mess Sir' and got myself out of trouble.[34]

There was some respite from combat, particularly when 2/6th Queens were pulled out of the line at Forlimpopoli. Bill received permission to go into Faenza and obtain supplies from the NAAFI. He hitched a ride by tank and came back in a Bren gun carrier laden with supplies. It was a joyous occasion returning to his company with luxuries such as pipe tobacco, writing materials, cakes and sweets which were much prized by his fellow infantrymen.

Early in 1945 Bill's luck eventually ran out. His battalion was tasked with the rescue of a wounded soldier stranded on the wrong side of the Senio. After the operation he was looking for some spare wireless batteries when caught in the open by enemy artillery fire. He was seriously wounded in the knee and groin but couldn't feel anything as he lay on the frozen ground.

Effectively, Bill's war was over. He was evacuated by air to Foggia and remained in hospital awaiting passage to Britain. However, while there he suffered a re-occurrence of malaria and was kept in Italy. One day a doctor hoisted him up and gave him an injection 'bang in my backside. And do you know I have never had the slightest reaction to malaria ever since but I couldn't sit down for a week!'[35]

Bill sailed into Liverpool on VE-Day unaware the Germans had surrendered. He was sent to hospital in Durham and then posted to a convalescent depot in Scarborough. Despite its benign-sounding name, this was an awful place 'full of warrant officers and sergeants swinging their lead'.[36] Young soldiers returning to duty from spells in hospital were put on route marches and punished for all kinds of offences.

Bill was relieved to receive another posting as the adjutant's clerk at an infantry depot in Gravesend. Subsequently, the remainder of his service was spent as an instructor at the Army college in Edinburgh. Here he taught typing to ATS girls and can still touch type to this day.

Bill Titchmarsh (centre wearing glasses) with some of his comrades from the Royal Hospital Chelsea during Armistice Day commemorations on Jersey. (Author's photograph)

After demob Bill received a pension of 13s 6d, later revoked by the Attlee government. He married and did a number of jobs, notably working as the manager secretary of a country club in the Home Counties. However, he remained proud of his war service often attending regimental reunions. Additionally, as a former member of the RMIJ he participates in Remembrance

Day and other ceremonies on Jersey. In late 2007 Bill was admitted as an in pensioner at the Royal Hospital, Chelsea. Here he is among a select and declining band of veterans who experienced life as wartime infantrymen and he recently enjoyed celebrating his ninetieth birthday.

Researching Bill Titchmarsh

Bill's campaign medals provided a starting point for researching his war service They clearly demonstrate he experienced combat overseas. He was awarded the 1939–45 Star; Africa Star (1st Army clasp); Italy Star; Defence Medal and 1939–45 War Medal. On being admitted to the Royal Hospital, Chelsea he was informed that he was ineligible for the Africa Star. He had only served seventy-nine days rather than the requisite ninety in that theatre. William Spencer's *Medals: The Researcher's Guide* (TNA, 2008) is an invaluable publication. Compiled by the chief military specialist at TNA, it provides advice on researching awards including those relevant to all three armed services during the Second World War. Similarly, wartime gallantry and campaign medals are covered by H. Taprell Dorling's *Ribbons and Medals*, ed. and rev. A. Purves (Osprey, 1983).

'Anzio"slaughterhouse"remembered' by Hannah Goff, *BBC News*, accessed at: www.http//newsvote.bbc.co.uk, 24 July 2005, neatly narrates Bill's sad story about his friend Willy. Additionally, a recording of Bill's reminiscences was made by the author at the Royal Hospital, Chelsea on 18 August 2010. This provided details of his Army service and wartime life in Southampton. When conducting interviews an informal style can work, especially with a relative as was the case here. Alternatively, it can prove beneficial to adopt a more structured approach using pre-arranged questions. Whatever method you deploy, try to avoid it becoming like an interrogation. Most people will be put off by this. Readers interested in conducting their own interviews should consult Trevor Lummis's *Listening to History* (Hutchinson, 1987) and Paul Thompson's *The Voice of the Past: Oral History* (Oxford University Press, 1988).

When researching an individual you may wish to consider their educational background. In Bill's case the Royal Merchant Navy School, now Bearwood College, has the following websites: www.bearwoodcollege.co.uk and www.oldroyals.org.uk. Most educational institutions will have some form of archive on old scholars, including those who served in the war, and you might wish to consider this in your own research.

Operational records relating to Bill's wartime service were consulted at TNA. Background on the RMIJ and its re-formation into 11th Battalion the Hampshire Regiment can be found in WO 32 General Series. The War Diary for the RMIJ is in WO 166 Home Forces and charts the movements and activities of that unit. War Diaries for 2/6th Queens, spanning the Italian Campaign 1943–5, are in WO 169 Middle East Forces and WO 170 Central Mediterranean Forces. These helped put Bill's experiences into context and would provide a suitable platform for further research into his war service and 2/6th Queens's part in the Italian Campaign.

Like many War Diaries, they contain much administrative detail, not all of which is relevant to an ordinary soldier. However, the Battalion Orders, including instructions on anti-malaria precautions, and Intelligence Summaries (Army Form C.2118), noting daily events, were particularly relevant to Bill's experience. Remember, these documents were often filled in retrospectively by battalion officers under pressure, so you will not necessarily find extensive detail on particular actions.

Additionally, WO 204 Allied Forces Mediterranean HQ Papers contains numerous reports on Italy, notably 'Operations at Anzio February–March 1944', a narrative compiled by 56th Division. When using TNA it is worth considering the mass of reports generated during wartime. While these will not usually deal with individuals, they will help you to place the personal experience of an individual into a wider framework. Always be prepared to trawl the online catalogue and don't be afraid of asking staff at Kew for assistance.

Major R. C. G. Foster MC, *History of the Queen's Regiment Vol. III 1924–48* (Gale & Polden Ltd, 1953) contains chapters describing 2/6th Queens's service in Italy in more detail. Regimental histories like this are expensive and difficult to obtain; always try the IWM (Department of Books) or the relevant regimental archive to see if they have copies. The Queen's Royal (West Surrey) Regiment, the oldest English infantry regiment, has a museum at Clandon Park, near Guildford, see: www.queensroyalsurreys.org.uk. However, since 2003 their regimental archive has been housed at the Surrey History Centre; for further information see: www.surreycc.gov.uk/surreyhistorycentre.

Dominick Graham and Shelford Bidwell's *Tug of War The Battle For Italy 1943–45* (Pen & Sword, 2004) provides a useful narrative of the Italian Campaign interlaced with analysis. Both men served as artillery officers and became widely respected military historians. John Ellis's *The Sharp End: The Fighting Man in World War II* (Pimlico, 1990) provides a thought-provoking chapter on infantry combat during the Second World War. Jeremy A. Crang's *The British Army and the People's War 1939–1945* (Manchester University Press, 2000) deals with the effects of wartime conscription upon the Army as a social institution. It discusses in detail issues such as officer selection and examines the role of institutions like the War Office Selection Board and Army Bureau of Current Affairs.

Churchill famously likened Anzio to a 'stranded whale' owing to Lucas's failure to break out from the beach-head given the level of materials landed there. However, as Bill's experiences demonstrate, for the troops involved it was one of the bloodiest battles of the war. The following provide useful reading: the *History of the Second World War* magazines by Purnell contain numerous articles on the Italian Campaign, notably Raleigh Trevelyan's 'Anzio-Blast & Counterblast', Vol. 4, No. 13, 1967. Martin Blumenson's *Anzio: The Gamble That Failed* (Weidenfeld & Nicolson, 1963) is written largely from an American perspective but is a readable narrative outlining the planning of Operation Shingle and conduct of subsequent battles in the beach-head. Christopher Hibbert's *Anzio: The Bid For Rome* (Macdonald, 1970) is a punchy account complemented by a good selection of photographs and line drawings.

Distinguished military historian and former soldier Carlo D'Este's *Fatal Decision: Anzio and the Battle for Rome* (Fontana, 1992) offers a comprehensive study. It is enriched by the author's analysis supported by evidence from various sources. Lloyd Clark's *Anzio: The Friction of War Italy and the Battle for Rome* (Headline Review, 2007) is eminently accessible and incorporates personal testimony of veterans from both sides of the conflict.

Notes

1. Jeremy A. Crang, *The British Army and the People's War 1939–1945* (Manchester University Press, 2000), p. 2.
2. 'Anzio "slaughterhouse" remembered' by Hannah Goff, *BBC News*, p. 1, accessed at: www.news.bbc.co.uk, 24 July 2005.
3. Author's interview with Bill Titchmarsh at the Royal Hospital, Chelsea, 18 August 2010.
4. Ibid.
5. Ibid.
6. Ibid.
7. Ibid.
8. Ibid.
9. TNA, WO 170/1466, War Diary 2/6th Bn Queens Royal Regt, Fontanelli, Intelligence Summary Entry, 12 February 1944.
10. Lloyd Clark, *Anzio: The Friction of War Italy and the Battle for Rome* (Headline Review, 2007), p. 321.
11. Author's interview with Bill Titchmarsh at the Royal Hospital, Chelsea, 18 August 2010.
12. Major R. C. G. Foster, MC, *History of the Queen's Regiment Vol. III 1924–48* (Gale & Polden Ltd, 1953), p. 289.
13. TNA, WO 204/8269, 56th London Division at Anzio, February–March 1944, p. 3.
14. Author's interview with Bill Titchmarsh at the Royal Hospital, Chelsea, 18 August 2010.
15. Ibid.
16. Foster, *History of the Queen's Regiment Vol. III 1924–48*, p. 293.
17. Author's interview with Bill Titchmarsh at the Royal Hospital, Chelsea, 18 August 2010.

18. Ibid.
19. Ibid.
20. Ibid.
21. 'Anzio "slaughterhouse" remembered' by Hannah Goff, *BBC News*, p. 2.
22. Author's interview with Bill Titchmarsh at the Royal Hospital, Chelsea, 18 August 2010.
23. Foster, *History of the Queen's Regiment Vol. III 1924–48*, p. 415.
24. TNA, WO 170/1466, War Diary 2/6th Bn Queens Royal Regt, Vis, Yugoslavia, Intelligence Summary Entry, 4 April 1944.
25. Ibid., Egypt, Intelligence Summary Entry, 16–30 June 1944.
26. Ibid., Italy, Intelligence Summary Entry, 26–31 July 1944.
27. Author's interview with Bill Titchmarsh at the Royal Hospital, Chelsea, 18 August 2010.
28. Ibid.
29. Ibid.
30. Ibid.
31. Ibid.
32. 'Anzio "slaughterhouse" remembered' by Hannah Goff, *BBC News*, p. 2.
33. Author's interview with Bill Titchmarsh at the Royal Hospital, Chelsea, 18 August 2010.
34. Ibid.
35. Ibid.
36. Ibid.

Chapter 8

To Battle by 'Flying Coffin' –
Albert 'Ginger' Wilson

Albert Wilson, 'Ginger', was born in Heysham, Lancashire in November 1923. On leaving school he worked in the grocery department of his local Co-Operative store. He then managed to gain employment as a tea boy for a gang of Irish labourers constructing a new ICI refinery. They each paid him 6*d* (2½ pence) so that at the end of a week he was able to take home £3, a considerable sum in the 1930s.

As soon as he was 16 Albert joined the Home Guard. He was instructed on the 'manufacture' of Molotov Cocktails for use against enemy armour. Theoretically, six bombs should have knocked out a tank once the flammable liquid seeped inside. To make them old beer bottles proved ideal. They were filled with equal amounts of tar and kerosene followed by a small measure of petrol. A piece of cloth was inserted in the neck as a wick.

When he was old enough Albert enlisted in the Regular Army on 18 June 1942. As Private A. Wilson No. 3608673, he was posted to 18 Infantry Training Company at Carlisle. This was the basic training organisation for the King's Own Royal Regiment, the Border Regiment and the Loyal Regiment. Here he would have done a considerable amount of 'square bashing', drill and musketry training.

He was then drafted to 7th Battalion the Border Regiment in Norfolk. That unit's primary task was to provide six weeks of further instruction to recruits fresh from basic training. In the barracks Albert saw a notice asking for volunteers to join 'the Airborne' and he decided to apply.

During 1940 a force of air-landing troops was formed which encouraged experiments with parachute jumping and gliders. When Albert volunteered the state of the airborne forces was more advanced. An airborne division comprised two parachute brigades, one air-landing brigade using gliders, plus supporting services. He was transferred to 1st Battalion the Border Regiment and joined B Company. The battalion was designated for glider-borne operations within 1st Air Landing Brigade from 1st Airborne Division. The gliders were comparatively flimsy and frequently referred to by soldiers as 'flying coffins'.[1]

The battalion was based at a comfortable, purpose-built camp in Barton Stacey, Hampshire. However, training was deliberately tough and those who failed to come up to standard were RTU'd (Returned To Unit). Not only was a high level of infantry training required, but physical fitness and mental stamina were vital too. Potentially, any airborne unit was liable to be deployed against targets behind enemy lines. Here they would have to fight unaided until support arrived.

Within 1st Border a training company operated for all new recruits like Albert. This included tasks such as 'run and walks'.[2] Troops in full kit with steel helmets and rifles were made alternately to run then walk the distance of two telegraph poles. Over several miles this could be exhausting. The entire battalion was involved in intensive training schemes throughout 1942–3 before being posted to North Africa. From there it was to take part in the Allied invasion of Sicily (Operation Husky).

The air component code-named Ladbroke preceded the amphibious assault. It was envisaged that 1st Border would land in the early hours of 10 July 1943 seize Syracuse and hold it until relieved by 5th Division the next day. Simultaneously, 2nd Battalion South Staffordshire Regiment was tasked with taking the key Ponte Grande bridge.

Everyone was cheerful. However, Albert experienced a strange feeling upon boarding his glider. He was well armed with a Bren gun, 8 spare magazines and 100 extra rounds about his person. For close protection he had a revolver, while a couple of grenades further weighed him down.

Ladbroke proved a disaster. Although a few gliders reached their objectives, most landed off course or ditched at sea. The Air Landing Brigade and Glider Pilot regiment suffered approximately 600 casualties, about half of whom drowned. The American-manufactured Waco Gliders were buffeted by 45mph winds over the Mediterranean. Albert recalled that many of the troops felt awful. Additionally, they were greeted by a hail of anti-aircraft fire approaching Sicily, having been towed a circuitous route via Malta.

Albert's glider was released too far out to maintain sufficient airspeed to reach land. It crashed at sea and rapidly filled with water. He managed to escape and perched on a wing. It had been a struggle to remove his boots and heavy equipment, particularly the grenades. Despite having blow-up life belts, most of the other soldiers stood little chance owing to the weight of their kit. Together with a few survivors he desperately clung to the semi-submerged glider during the night. They sang songs to keep warm and stave off hypothermia.

In daylight they discovered that they were about 5 miles off Syracuse Harbour. Fortunately, friendly vessels from the invasion fleet were in the vicinity. One picked them up. However, it was unable to stop owing to enemy action and the exhausted soldiers had to grab ropes and be hauled aboard as she passed.

Later, Albert and other survivors were shipped to Malta. Here a doctor threw a hypodermic into their buttocks much in the manner of a darts player. This was to inoculate them against the risk of infection picked up from the sea. When he had recuperated Albert was posted back to North Africa. Here his unit was recovering from the Ladbroke debacle. The total killed, wounded, injured and missing in 1st Border was 9 officers and 180 other ranks.

In December 1943 Albert sailed back to the Britain aboard the *Duchess of Bedford*. She was christened the 'Drunken Duchess' on account of her tendency to roll.[3] His battalion was posted to Lincolnshire, where he met a local girl whom he later married. Airborne units were now busily preparing for the much vaunted 'Second Front'. As 6th Airborne Division was given priority for

A wartime portrait of Lance Corporal Albert 'Ginger' Wilson, 11 Platoon, B Company, 1st Battalion the Border Regiment.
(Cumbria's Military Museum)

D-Day, 1st Airborne Division remained on standby. This entailed extensive training and was frustrating. Frequently, prospective operations were cancelled and Albert was not in action again until 17 September 1944.

Early that month Montgomery had persuaded Eisenhower that the Allied advance into Germany could be hastened via an ambitious airborne offensive code-named Operation Market. This would seize key bridges over the Maas, Waal and Rhine that enabled Operation Garden, a thrust by British 2nd Army spearheaded by XXX Corps, to occur. The British 1st Airborne Division and a Polish parachute brigade were tasked with securing Arnhem.

Numerous problems arose. Owing to shortages of aircraft, the drops had to be made over three days which allowed the Germans time to recover. The enemy had more panzer forces near Arnhem than previously thought. Unfortunately, plans for the entire operation were found on a dead American officer. At Arnhem the British had to be dropped 7 miles from the Rhine bridge to avoid enemy anti-aircraft guns. These same guns were effectively deployed against later lifts. Bad weather hampered the fly-in of supplies and reinforcements. British units were hindered by the absence of an effective long-range radio. The hastily cobbled together air plan by 2nd Tactical Air Force failed to provide close air support consistently.

Ultimately, the enemy was able to contain the advance by 2nd Army and prevent it linking with 1st Airborne Division. Simultaneously, they tightened the noose around the isolated British and Poles at Arnhem who courageously fought on. After an epic nine-day battle 1st Airborne Division had lost an estimated 7,000 men and only around 2,400 made it back across the Rhine.

In preparation for Market 1st Border were posted to Burford, Oxfordshire. Albert and his mates were 'amused' to find themselves barracked in pigsties. He boarded his Horsa glider in good spirits. Briefings had alluded to the supposed weakness of the German forces in Holland.

The flight was comparatively comfortable in bright sunshine. However, at the landing zone it was confused and tense. Several gliders had collided with one another and his stopped only 10yd from a copse. On jumping out he saw a glider suspended 40ft up some trees. The 6-pounder anti-tank gun it carried having smashed through the cockpit killing both pilots, whose bodies now hung in the branches.

Albert's platoon sergeant was carried away wounded from the wreckage of another glider. He found himself promoted to section leader. Together with Private Frank Aston, he was ordered to take a PIAT (Projector Infantry Anti-Tank) and 'stop any trains coming from Arnhem'.[4] Fortunately, none came. At this stage the air-landing brigade was securing the drop zones for the second lift on 18 September. Albert remembered having 'a grandstand view of the Para's dropping, it was a magnificent sight'.[5]

After the drop Major Tom Armstrong's B Company including Albert's Number 11 Platoon moved on Renkum. Their aim was to block the main Utrecht road leading to Oosterbeek and Arnhem. Everything went well and the troops advanced 'down the main street into Renkum, in single file'.[6] Then a German lorry with a machine gun managed to get among them but it was rapidly shot up.

The platoon dug in on the river bank near the wall of a brick works with the rest of the company within the works itself. That evening Albert's section was ordered to lay an ambush for sixty German cycle troops approaching Renkum.

> The house we picked had two old gentlemen in bed upstairs. When we went in the big bedroom Frank and I started to explain to them what we were doing and that German soldiers were coming. By then we had got the windows open, with Bren mags and 36 grenades [The standard grenade was the Number 36] on the window sills. We then started to jump about as if we had been shot, they must have thought us a right bunch of nut cases! In the end we got them out of bed, put some clothes on and sent them downstairs. The rest of my section were . . . in the ground floor rooms. I'll always remember their long night shirts, and the long pointed hats they were wearing.[7]

The section stayed until word came from the Dutch Resistance that the Germans had taken another route into town.

They returned to their trenches only to find that by morning the Germans occupied nearby houses. Several appeared in front of Albert's position. He 'gave Frank a nudge and he put a full Bren mag into them. They then pinned us down on the river bank.'[8] Number 11 Platoon acted as the rearguard to allow the rest of B Company to escape. Lieutenant S. Barnes, Albert's platoon commander, asked if his section would be the last out and cover the platoon's withdrawal:

> When our platoon had gone I told my section to dump everything but their ammo. You can't eat if your dead I told them . . . Frank and I covered the riflemen with the Bren because we had about 30 yards of open ground before getting down to the river bank. We gave the section about 15 minutes, then made a dash. It's a miracle we weren't hit. When we had run about 300 yards, I crept up the river bank to

look, I nearly had a heart attack as 100 Germans were launching a full frontal attack on our positions. We ran like hell and just got to the woods [at Westerbouwing] as the Germans got to the top of the river bank.[9]

Later 11 Platoon dug in along the Oosterbeekseweg, the road from Heveadorp. They were surprised to discover a warehouse full of German machine guns. Frustratingly, no ammunition could be found for these to be deployed against their former owners.

During 20/21 September 11 Platoon fought off enemy attacks and intense fire fights developed. Albert and Frank could hear Germans creeping around their trench that night and 'fired over 100 rounds into them'.[10] A German machine-gunner narrowly missed them both but then succeeded in hitting Frank's helmet with his second burst. They returned fire and the German appeared to be silenced. The ferocity of the fighting can be gauged by the fact that after 20 minutes they had run out of ammunition.

Albert decided they should head for the platoon HQ at a nearby hotel and obtain more ammunition:

As we ran somebody fired from our left and hit Frank and missed me. His dying words were 'Oh Ginger Oh' as he lay in my arms. I picked him up and the Bren and ran to the hotel . . . I was laid beside my dead mate. He was like a brother to me, we loved to play football together. It was the saddest day of my life.[11]

Albert put Frank's personal effects in his left breast pocket hoping give them to his mother on returning to Britain.

At dawn the platoon faced another assault as the Germans attempted to deal with the Oosterbeek perimeter. The men could hear tanks approaching and soon opened up with every available weapon. Albert's Bren jammed so he desperately attempted to free the cocking handle with the base of a hand grenade and eject the empty cartridge. Simultaneously, the soldier next to him, 'a nice lad from Cumberland', was shot through the middle of the forehead.[12]

With the enemy only 40yd away they tried once again to rejoin the rest of their company. Albert passed a wounded German of similar age who he sensed was equally as scared as he was. As they were being overrun, the company commander ordered a barrage on their positions. Coupled with enemy tank fire, this was a terrifying ordeal and incoming rounds felt 'like a welding flash on your eyes'.[13]

As the fighting progressed, B Company became mixed up. A small group under Lieutenant Barnes, including Albert, dug in near a big house called Dennenoord. It was a good defensive position high up that commanded open ground to the front. At night attempts were made to take the ferry at Westerbouwing but met stubborn German resistance. A corporal next to Albert received a burst of machine-gun fire to the face. He was forced to escape the Germans via sodden dykes and return to the comparative safety of Dennenoord.

By now enemy snipers had worked their way into the nearby gas works. Mortar and artillery bombardments were frequent. Albert recalled, 'there were branches all over, blown off the trees, it was complete devastation in front of Dennenoord'.[14] He was sickened by the sight of the wounded, particularly a young soldier with the 'handle of German stick grenade embedded in his elbow'.[15] He witnessed a soldier in the next trench who 'got a piece of shrapnel straight through the top of his helmet. The lad with him was just sat there suffering from shell shock.'[16]

Rumours emerged that a withdrawal across the river was planned for 25/26 September. Albert was standing in the garage at Dennenoord with Lieutenant Barnes and four other soldiers discussing the news. Suddenly, a shell landed that seriously wounded Barnes in the foot and killed the soldiers. Albert was left unscathed. He carried Barnes to the medics in the cellar and staunched the flow of blood from the foot with his smock.

Clearly, Barnes was in no state to cross the river. Instead, Albert had to accompany another wounded officer. Several men gave him their addresses in case he made it to safety. However, at the river bank it was chaos. Rather than remain easy targets for the Germans they headed back to Dennenoord. There a tall Dutch lady made Albert leave his gun outside and shortly afterwards they heard German voices.

On being captured he was offered Senior Service cigarettes, probably from one of the Allied airdrops that had gone awry. Initially, he was told to help the Germans look for wounded. Then with other prisoners he was taken to the Hartenstein Hotel and made to pick up litter. This was in fact paper from documents ripped up by 1st Airborne Division's HQ before they withdrew.

The POWs were marched into Arnhem and put in a large house for the night. En route they passed several dead whose heads were grotesquely swollen so that 'their helmets were like those little policemen's hats you can buy at the seaside, that just sit on top of your head'.[17] Albert was thankful that he was still alive, although the full shock of captivity was yet to sink in.

Extract from the Border Regiment POW Register showing Albert's details, including his Army No. 3608673. This is a good example of the type of document regimental museums may hold that will assist the family historian. (Author's photograph)

On 28 September he was herded into a cattle truck minus his boots to prevent escape. He ended up at a transit camp, Stalag XIIA at Limburg. Here he had his first 'meal' since eating cherries at Dennenoord. It was dehydrated soup from the 1930s with maggots floating on top. Even for a starving soldier this was difficult to stomach.

Albert was issued with a postcard to tell his family that he was a POW and in good health. This did not arrive until January 1945. Instead, his fiancée heard about his predicament via one of Lord Haw-Haw's broadcasts boasting of the destruction of British forces at Arnhem.

The Germans soon forced him to work by unloading concrete slabs from railway wagons. This had some advantages. Once a wagon of apples spilled its load and these were swapped with Russian prisoners for bread. Another task was loading flour onto trucks, which again had its compensations. One bag burst covering the German guards much to the amusement of the POWs.

Back at camp Albert retaliated by telling his interrogating officer how marvellous the food was back in Britain. The German ended up salivating with envy. Subsequently, he was transported to Stalag Luft III at Sagan, East Germany, a permanent camp run by the Luftwaffe with barrack huts and barbed wire. En route they were offered apples by a German. Lacking anything else of value Albert handed over Frank's cigarette case. He had been keeping it for his mother and felt guilt stricken about this for many years.

At Sagan Albert's hut had no windows or beds and much time was spent trying to scavenge for firewood. He was eternally grateful to other British POWs who shared Red Cross parcels with him. It was possible to barter cigarettes and chocolate with German guards for potatoes. Even so, the POWs were perpetually hungry. To add to his misery Albert seriously scalded his arm when boiling potatoes. The medical hut could only provide Vaseline. Eventually, it healed helped by a kind elderly German guard who let him stay in bed and miss roll calls.

One bright spot was the arrival of a Christmas Red Cross parcel. Albert's hut made a 'banquet' out of the Huntley & Palmer cake it contained. Then in early 1945 he was part of a group marched out of Sagan in bitter cold towards Czechoslovakia. This lasted about three weeks and stragglers were left to die. Once a Polish girl ran up to give them crusts of bread. Albert was disturbed to learn that after the war she and her friends were shot by the Russians as collaborators.

They were taken to Bad Orb Stalag near Frankfurt having witnessed many horrors. Notably, the suffering caused when an Allied fighter strafed another column of POWs believing them to be Germans. Most POWs were painfully thin and exhausted. At the camp conditions were appalling with frequent deaths. In desperation the padre asked POWs to check the linings of their clothes for aspirin or vitamin tablets. To make matters even worse an American fighter unfortunately shot up nearby railway wagons. These contained Red Cross parcels destined for the camp.

At Easter 1945 the camp was liberated by American troops. Albert was flown back to Britain to begin the path to recovery. Initially, he was given a large meal that made him violently ill. Later, he thought that this must have been deliberate so as to get all the 'Stalag stuff' out of his system. His mother and sweetheart helped by caring for him and feeding him eggs, milk and fish. On VE-Day he was heading home towards Heysham with his sweetheart from Lincolnshire.

However, the Army had not finished with him yet. In June 1945 he was medically downgraded and briefly served with 2nd Lancashire Fusiliers before being transferred to the RAOC. After completing a course in Yorkshire, he received a posting to RAOC Wilford Brickyard, Nottinghamshire. Work was dull and consisted of checking over motorbikes. Albert was also suffering from headaches and mood swings. His wartime soldiering had left him with what today would probably be termed a form of combat stress.

Having gone AWOL (Absent Without Leave), he was sent to see an Army doctor and was hospitalised in Birmingham. At the Lord Nuffield Mental Institution he found some solace in playing for their football team. As he put it, 'while I was kicking hell out of a football, I wasn't doing it to anyone else'.[18] Eventually, Albert was demobbed in December 1945. He received a pension of 7s a week for two years and 1s when his first son was born.

Having settled in Lincolnshire, Albert married his sweetheart and they ran a small holding which helped him forget the horrors of war. She was a tower of strength in enabling him come to terms with his wartime experiences. As he recalled:

> For nearly two years every time I put my hands to my mouth to eat, I could smell human blood and cordite and nightmares for a good five years. I used to see a bullet coming straight between my eyes, on impact I used to wake up sweat pouring off me. None of my relations knew anything about these things only [my wife]. . . she brought sanity back into my life.[19]

As a widower in later life, he gained comfort from maintaining contact with old comrades from the Border Regiment and enjoyed visiting Arnhem with them.

Researching Albert Wilson

Researching Albert's war service was made easier because he served predominantly with one unit. Visits to Cumbria's Military Museum (Border Regiment and King's Own Royal Border Regiment) at Carlisle Castle enabled me to access specific documents regarding 1st Battalion the Border Regiment. The War Diary, c. 1943–4, provided substantial operational detail on Sicily and

Arnhem. Albert's brief entries in the Enlistment Register and Regimental POW Record Book added a personal touch and confirmed his basic details. Additionally, the museum holds extensive files of correspondence with veterans including Albert. These give an insight into wartime training, operational and personal experience.

There were two articles held by the museum that proved helpful: Captain N. A. H. Stafford's 'Operation "Husky" 1st Battalion Prepare for the Assault on Sicily' in *Border Magazine*, March 1954 and Major J. D. Gibbon MC's 'Operation "Husky" Part II' in *Border Magazine*, September 1954. Remember when corresponding with regimental museums that it is advisable to enclose an SAE. Be patient as most lack the resources to handle enquiries instantaneously and always check their websites when planning a visit.

TNA hold extensive records on wartime airborne units. Although not of a genealogical nature, these will provide much detail on operations. Reports on Operation Husky and the Mediterranean can be found in WO 106 and WO 204. Information regarding Market Garden is contained within WO 361 and WO 205. War Diaries for 1st Border Regiment covering service in Britain and overseas 1943–5 are in WO 166, WO 169 and WO 175. Additionally, with someone like Albert who was captured it is worth trawling through WO 344 Liberated POW Questionnaires. Besides basic information such as name, rank and number, these list camps, medical treatment, punishments, escapes and work parties etc.

Albert's wartime experiences are well covered by his unpublished memoirs. These give vivid descriptions of infantry combat at section level. Copies are held by the SWWEC, Cumbria's Military Museum and the IWM. Additionally, SWWEC holds a copy of Colonel J. L. Waddy OBE, 'A Soldier's Story' in *British Army Review*, No. 114, an article based on Albert's memoirs. Similarly, Jim Longson and Christine Taylor's *An Arnhem Odyssey* (Leo Cooper, 1991) draws upon Albert's experiences and provides information on his early life.

The *Home Guard Manual 1941*, reprinted by Tempus Publishing Ltd (2006), provides substantial details on the training of that organisation. Philip J. Shears's *The Story of the Border Regiment 1939–1945* (Nisbet & Co. Ltd, 1948) and Stuart Eastwood, Charles Gray and Alan Green's *When Dragons Flew An Illustrated History of The 1st Battalion The Border Regiment 1939–45* (Regimental Museum in association with Silver Link Publishing Ltd, 2009) put Albert's experiences into context. Regimental histories and wartime manuals can sometimes be obtained from museums, second-hand book shops or via the Internet. Alternatively, it is well worth consulting the IWM, NAM or relevant regimental archives.

Carlo D'Este's *Bitter Victory: The Battle For Sicily 1943* (Fontana, 1989) provides an authoritative account of Operation Husky, including the airborne aspect. There are numerous narratives available on the controversial Operation Market Garden and the following are a suggested guide from a British perspective: Stephen Badsey's *Arnhem 1944* (Osprey Publishing, 1993) is a lavishly illustrated and concise account in the 'Osprey Campaign Series'. Martin Middlebrook's *Arnhem 1944 The Airborne Battle* (Penguin Books, 1995) is a comprehensive account that refers to Albert and his battalion. Lloyd Clark's *Arnhem Jumping the Rhine 1944 and 1945 The Greatest Airborne Battle in History* (Headline Review, 2009) is another accessible book featuring the personal testimony of several veterans including Albert. Major General R. E. Urquhart CB, DSO, *Arnhem* (Pan Books, 1972) and Cornelius Ryan's classic work *A Bridge Too Far* (Book Club Associates, 1975) are pithy, general accounts for anyone interested in the battle. Material on Arnhem can also be viewed at: www.pegasusarchive.org, but be warned Internet content is unedited and should generally be treated with caution.

Notes

1. Carlo D'Este, *Bitter Victory: The Battle for Sicily 1943* (Fontana, 1989), p. 228.
2. Stuart Eastwood, Charles Gray and Alan Green, *When Dragons Flew An Illustrated History of The 1st Battalion The Border Regiment 1939–45* (Silver Link Publishing Ltd, 2009), p. 34.
3. Ibid., p. 93.
4. Cumbria's Military Museum, Albert 'Ginger' Wilson, untitled manuscript re Arnhem experiences, p. 1.
5. Ibid.
6. Ibid.
7. Ibid., pp. 1–2.
8. Ibid., pp. 2–3.
9. Ibid., p. 2.
10. Ibid., pp. 2–3.
11. Ibid., p. 3.
12. Ibid., p. 4.
13. Ibid.
14. Ibid., p. 7.
15. Ibid.
16. Ibid., p. 6.
17. Ibid., p. 10.
18. Second World War Experience Centre, Acc. No. LEEWW/2004-2705, Albert 'Ginger' Wilson, typed manuscript 'After the Battle', p. 17.
19. Ibid., p. 18.

Chapter 9

A Spitfire Pilot Over the Mediterranean – James Anthony Tooth

Tony Tooth was one of those pilots fortunate enough to have flown the Spitfire, that iconic aircraft of the Second World War. However, as a boy it seemed that he was destined to follow in his father's footsteps and join the Navy. He was born in November 1922 and shortly after his family moved to Bembridge on the Isle of Wight. During his childhood he witnessed all types of naval vessels, ocean liners and aircraft while playing on the beach. This included the Supermarine S.6B, winner of the 1931 Schneider Trophy, which may have inspired him to later join the RAF.

Tony's father was made redundant as result of inter-war defence cuts and entered the Church. Eventually, the family settled at Rowner, a small village near Gosport. Tony was educated at a small preparatory school in Kent then Haileybury College during the late 1930s.

At 17 he tried to enter the Navy but his medical in the spring of 1940 demonstrated that he was colour-blind. This was a severe blow but he was able to serve in the LDV, forerunner of the Home Guard, as his school had formed a detachment based on their cadet corps, 'It was a great thrill to have a rifle and bayonet by ones bedside. I will never forget the great glee with which the two old sergeants, who ran the armoury, attacked the task of putting a razor edge on all the bayonets in the armoury.'[1]

Leaving school and returning to Rowner, Tony served in another LDV detachment on the south coast. He had a grandstand view of aerial actions during the Battle of Britain, particularly attacks by Junkers Ju 87 Stuka dive-bombers. In November, once he was 18 he joined the RAF at a recruiting office in Portsmouth.

They classified him as '"Colour defective safe-safe…" "safe" to fly aeroplanes, but my RAF driving licence was endorsed in red ink "not to be employed on airfield duties!"'[2] He felt, perhaps on account of his public-school background, as if he was rushed through the system. During December he attended a RW at Babbacombe, Devon, where he was initiated into 'RAF life' and issued with his uniform.

From there he was posted to an ITW at nearby Paignton for RAF basic training. Typically, ITWs were set up in coastal resorts away from areas suffering from enemy bombing and where accommodation was plentiful. Recruits were drilled extensively and received instruction on topics such as navigation and the theory of flight. The food and billets were poor but the lectures were held in a mansion that had belonged to the Singer family.

After completing basic training, Tony remained at Paignton eagerly awaiting his turn to progress with flying training. In the spring of 1941 he was selected for flying training in the USA. This promised an exciting break from the 'barrack-like' ITW routine. Having endured an unpleasant transit camp in Wilmslow, recruits were issued with a motley collection of khaki tropical uniforms and transported by rail to the Clyde. Here they boarded the *Royal Ulsterman*, a ferry that supplied the British garrison in Iceland where they spent three weeks in a camp run by an eccentric, elderly squadron leader.

From there they were transported to North America aboard HMS *Circassia*, an armed merchant cruiser deployed to patrol between Iceland and Nova Scotia. Eventually they trained at No. 1 British Flying Training School (No. 1 BFTS), Love Field, Dallas. This relied on the Dallas School of Aviation to provide instructors and facilities, while aircraft were supplied by the American military.

Here Tony first encountered the Boeing Stearman, a two-seat biplane trainer of inter-war vintage.

> The flying proved very enjoyable and at times very exciting, apart from learning how to get the aeroplane off the ground, and down again, there were important things like navigation, formation flying and aerobatics that are vital for the military pilot to master. The reason for this is that a military pilot has to be able to make an aircraft do anything that it is physically capable of.[3]

Tony progressed to a basic flying course at Terrell, east of Dallas using the Vultee Valiant, a sturdy looking monoplane that marked a significant technological step up from the Stearman. Tony found it 'a handsome but ill-mannered beast' on which to complete 40 hours of basic flight training.[4]

Subsequently, advanced flight training was conducted on the even more awe-inspiring North American AT6, a single-engine monoplane trainer designated the Harvard in RAF service. This 'was really a very nice aircraft to fly, although if treated carelessly or without due respect, it could bite, and bite very quickly and very hard'.[5]

It was in an aging Boeing PT 18 Stearman like this one that Tony Tooth gained his first flying experience while stationed in the USA. (Author's photograph)

On completing flight training Tony earned the right to wear the much-coveted RAF flying badge or 'Wings'. Unfortunately, those for his course and a letter from the Air Ministry authorising personnel to wear badges of rank didn't arrive. Even so, to have passed flight training was a great achievement. He was dispatched to a transit camp at Moncton, New Brunswick, where he celebrated his nineteenth birthday, before sailing in a convoy from Halifax, Nova Scotia bound for Liverpool.

Once in Britain Tony received a one-month posting to No. 5 FTS at Tern Hill, Shropshire. Here he flew the Miles Master, an advanced trainer that was the British equivalent of the AT6, and intended to prepare pilots for high-performance monoplanes like the Spitfire. He recalled 'we learned the RAF way of doing things and tried to find our way around the murky British skies'.[6]

Having adjusted to British flying conditions, Tony was pleased to be posted to fly Mk 1 and 2 Spitfires with No. 61 OTU based near London. Many of the other pilots were amiable Battle of Britain veterans and flying such a fighter became a delight. By April 1942 he had gained enough experience for a full operational posting and was dispatched to No. 130 (Punjab) Squadron stationed in Cornwall.

The squadron was sometimes involved in sweeps over northern France designed to provoke the Luftwaffe, and personnel experienced limited action on interception sorties or as convoy escorts. However, this was predominantly a quiet sector and the squadron's primary purpose was to provide recently qualified pilots with practice of combat flying. Accordingly, training emphasised topics such as formation flying, tactics, gunnery and simulated dog fights.

Having gained experience with No. 130 Squadron, Tony was posted to the Hurricane equipped No. 175 Squadron in Dorset. Formed in March 1942, the squadron had been conducting anti-shipping strikes and coastal patrols and was earmarked for deployment in Operation Torch (Allied Landings in French North Africa, 8 November 1942). This would require him to convert to the Hurricane which he infinitely disliked and considered clumsy when compared with the more elegant Spitfire. Luckily for him, No. 175 Squadron was removed from the plan.

Consequently, Tony was able to fly Spitfires again when posted to No. 152 (Hyderabad) Squadron. This was the squadron with which he would experience significant combat flying. It had been re-formed in October 1939 and conducted various duties around Britain, including helping protect the south coast during the Battle of Britain.

When Tony joined in late 1942 the squadron had just moved to RAF Wittering, a Bomber Command base ahead of a deployment overseas. They were to serve in North Africa flying the latest models of Spitfire, the Mk VB with two 20mm cannon and four guns and Mk VC with the 'universal wing' which could take the above armament or four cannon. Both were capable of carrying a 500lb (113kg) bomb load, normally divided into two 250lb bombs.[7] They were converted into 'tropical' configuration with 'a huge and ugly air filter under the nose in an attempt to keep out the clouds of sand we would encounter'.[8]

The air resources deployed during Operation Torch were intended cut off the enemy's line of retreat in French North Africa and so assist friendly ground forces. Despite their defeats in the desert, German ground and air units demonstrated plenty of fighting spirit. Additionally, pilots like Tony were faced with awkward conditions and 'handicapped both by poor logistic and maintenance facilities and . . . a lack of suitable airfields'.[9]

At Souk al Arba, where the squadron spent a few months, there were 'two worn-out tents borrowed from the Foreign Legion, one pick-up truck, one very enterprising young airman and a bunch of "servicing commandos" who kept the aircraft flying'.[10] Mud was a particular bugbear for the Spitfire on such a primitive airfield. As Tony explained, 'because of the very heavy engine sticking out so far in front that it is liable to tip over on its nose, breaking the propeller, also the propeller whips up mud and plasters it into the radiator, blocking it and causing the engine to overheat'.[11]

Additionally, flying out to Tunisia was a feat of endurance, even in a high-performance aircraft like the Spitfire and tragically No. 152 Squadron lost a pilot en route. On arrival pilots were confronted by the 'most incredibly congested airfield imaginable, apart from its normal complement of French and German civil aircraft it was absolutely packed with British and American fighter, bomber, and transport types, chaos'.[12]

There was no air traffic control and soon Tony experienced a near miss. It was his first night landing in a Spitfire:

> luckily I did a bad landing and immediately left the runway on to the grass, as I did so [an American] B 26 Marauder bomber came past me doing at least 125 m.p.h. to my 75. He had seen me but was determined to get down first . . . the Spit was not a nice plane to fly at night as the engine produced spectacular amounts of flame . . . in the direction the pilot would be looking when landing . . . after that little incident I didn't see a new bomb crater in the dark and went straight into it.[13]

He had another narrow escape when his undercarriage collapsed forcing him to crash land as he strove to avoid a bomb-disposal crew working on the runway. Fortunately, the 90-gallon extra fuel tank he was carrying failed to explode. The cockpit filled with noxious fumes but luckily a rescue crew was on hand to evacuate him swiftly.

During December 1942 Tony experienced his first action against the Luftwaffe. He recalled wasting ammunition when trying to fire at a Messerschmitt Bf 109 at long range. The next day his squadron was attacked by a large number of enemy fighters that precipitated a confused dog fight.

> I know that I was attacked by a 109 and that I nearly ran into a FW 190, there appeared to be dozens of aircraft milling around me then suddenly, miraculously, the air was empty . . . characteristic of aerial combat that many pilots have remarked on. I found myself at 22,000 feet, all alone and over enemy territory and knowing there were many enemies around, there is only one thing to do under those circumstances . . . go home as fast as you can . . . right down on the deck, as low as you dare fly.[14]

On landing the ground crew showed him a bullet hole in his engine cowling but fortunately the round had not hit anything vital.

As the campaign progressed No. 152 Squadron were deployed as escort for slower flying Bisley bombers (later named Blenheim Mk V) against enemy targets. Owing to their slow speeds, this was an unpopular chore but a necessary one as the bombers were defenceless without fighter cover. Tony was to have yet another close shave when returning from escorting the bombers on 7 December as his airfield was strafed and bombed by a group of Focke Wulf 190s. It was frightening being caught in the open like that, 'one pilot was killed by bomb splinters about fifty yards from me and two planes completely destroyed'.[15]

Tony was fortunate to be given leave over Christmas 1942 and spent it in the mountains where to his surprise he found the hotel's chef had previously worked at Claridge's in London. By February the squadron had moved to a new airfield at Souk al Kheims to the east which was better equipped to cope with Spitfires. They continued to fly on bomber escort sorties and Tony was to experience another drawback of the Spitfire. If only one cannon fired, the recoil was so vicious that it would rock the entire aircraft making aiming impossible.

The Spitfires were also being deployed in a fighter-bomber role which prompted the squadron to develop suitable tactics. As Tony outlined:

we would go over at 10,000 feet, out of range of the light guns, roll into a 60 degree dive, aim at the target over the nose, hold it to around 4 or 5,000 feet or until the aircraft started to get unmanageable due to high speed (around 450 m.p.h.) then lift the nose to just cover the target, press the bomb release and ease the aircraft out of the dive.[16]

As the Tunisian campaign progressed Tony continued to face the hazards of combat flying. Not only was the enemy a threat but accidents posed an ever present danger, particularly during take-off and landing in the harsh conditions. Once his aircraft was damaged so severely by ground fire that an entire wing had to be replaced, something the ground crew achieved very efficiently so he could fly the next day.

Tony continued to garner experience both of air-to-air combat and when operating in the fighter-bomber role. Then on 10 May he contracted dysentery and was evacuated to a hospital in Constantine. Fortunately, drugs were available to combat this condition and he recovered rapidly and was discharged. At a transit camp near Algiers he was relieved to receive a posting back to his former squadron. They were now in Malta supporting the Allied invasion of Sicily (Operation Husky, 9 July 1943).

While on patrol on 12 July he spotted a twin-engined Messerschmitt Me 110 low over Gela and pursued the enemy fighter, despite carrying long-range fuel tanks that had to be jettisoned to improve his speed. No. 152 Squadron's Operational Record Book explains what happened next:

> Flying Officer Tooth who made a forced landing in Sicily on 12 July returned to the unit today. After firing all his ammunition at a Me 110 without observing any results he was obliged to make a forced landing near Gela due to a glycol leak [causing his engine to overheat]. He lay up from 9.30 hours until dark in a ditch and then made his way back to the coast where he contacted an American Unit.[17]

Once in Malta Tony was soon in action again as his squadron took part in the efforts being made to thwart the German withdrawal from Sicily to mainland Italy.

> I got in a good shot at fairly long range at a Bf 109 which slowed him down considerably and allowed me to catch up, difficult with a 109G as they were faster than the Spit 5. When I caught up I found my usual problem, one cannon not working, so I sat behind him and fired off a lot of ammunition in vain.
>
> I then put my thinking cap on and decided that I wasn't in a very invidious position and it would be better if I cleared off. I was on my own, short of ammunition and unable to shoot straight, my opponent badly damaged and probably unable to get home, so I rolled over, dived down to sea level and set off home. I had quite a long way to go, over open sea to start with, then either through the Messina Straight, not highly recommended as it had one of the highest concentrations of anti-aircraft guns in the world, or overland round west of Etna, further, but preferable under the circumstances. First I had the open sea to cover, . . . as I flew low over the water enormous splashes appeared in front . . . it took a moment for me to realise what was happening. I was straight off Cap Milazzo where there was a coast defence battery of eight inch guns which fired huge shells and they were trying to drop them in front of me![18]

Tony's squadron continued to act as escort for bombers, particularly medium models like the American B-25 Mitchell and B-26 Marauder. This was unpopular work as the slow speed of the bombers ensured the Spitfires were often at a disadvantage when jumped by enemy fighters. The RAF pilots much preferred escorting P-40 Kittyhawk fighter-bombers, the performance of which was more comparable to that of the Spitfires.

Personnel from No. 152 Squadron RAF, including Tony Tooth (initialled 'T.T.'), Malta, June 1943.
(SWWEC)

During August–September 1943 No. 152 Squadron began re-equipping with the Mk IX Spitfire, effectively an upgraded version of the Mk VC capable of matching the German FW 190A. Tony only flew the MK IX Spitfire once before being informed that his operational tour was over and he was to depart for HQ Middle East in Cairo.

From there he received a posting to Rhodesia (now Zimbabwe) where he was to undertake a course at No. 33 Flying Instructor's School, Norton. This fostered a lifelong love affair with Africa. However, during the war he found the attitude of personnel at Norton unfriendly, particularly when contrasted with the camaraderie of a front-line fighter squadron. This was partly due to the differences in attitude between pilots who had flown operationally and those who had not. Tony was fortunate that his instructor was the only pilot with operational experience and so had a positive attitude towards him. Trainees had to:

> demonstrate any manoeuvre impeccably . . . without any risk of it going wrong, whilst at the same time explaining it clearly and accurately. Not the easiest of things to do. Maintaining the Patter, as the talk was called, through any exercise not going according to plan could be a real challenge, calling for ingenuity and a bit of cheek.[19]

The North American AT-6 or T-6 Texan was one of the most important training aircraft of the war with more than 20,000 being manufactured either in the USA or under licence abroad. In British and Commonwealth service it was known as the Harvard. (Author's photograph)

Tony predominantly flew the Harvard and the course lasted until January 1944. He was delighted to qualify and be passed as suitable to instruct unsupervised and receive promotion to flight lieutenant with the accompanying pay rise. Subsequently, he was posted to No. 20 Service Flying School (No. 20 SFS) at Cranborne, near Salisbury.

Flying in the clear Rhodesian skies was an exhilarating experience, especially when there were hoards of game to be spotted. However, Tony had mixed views about his new job:

there were definite highlights of great satisfaction at times, but mostly very boring routine, punctuated by some very frightening moments. The frights almost all came when teaching new students to land in the Harvard MK. I, old and battered machines that had minds of their own and could be quite vicious. One certainly had to keep on ones toes.[20]

114

The Air Ministry stipulated that aircrew working at an altitude of 5,000ft, as in Rhodesia, were to be given annual leave at sea level to recuperate. During his leave Tony visited Cape Town and adored its vibrancy. The war in Europe ended while he was there. He was still there on VJ-Day and witnessed the wild celebrations in the streets. Eventually, he made it back to Britain aboard a comfortable liner, which was in stark contrast to the troopships he had been used to.

Tony was posted to 287 Squadron at RAF West Malling operating the high-performance Hawker Tempest and Spitfire Mk XVI. Post-war flying was dull but at least he was flying given that so many pilots now faced redundancy. After a month he was selected to become a ferry pilot, which proved exciting as it gave him an opportunity to fly various types of aircraft. This included the de Havilland Vampire, an early British jet fighter, and several Navy aircraft that would not normally be experienced by RAF pilots.

In July 1946 he left the RAF after six years' service and was given a gratuity of £186 (equivalent to about £4,000 today) plus his demob suit. Initially, he moved to London to take stock of things but later spent many years back in Rhodesia. He was immensely proud to have served in the wartime RAF and fondly remembers the generosity shown by many famous pilots, even to those of comparatively lowly rank like himself.

Researching James Anthony Tooth

Tony Tooth's wartime service, including his 'escape' after being forced to crash-land in Sicily, can be read in more detail in his unpublished twenty-page memoir, a copy of which is held by SWWEC. Another source of similar memoirs is the IWM (Department of Documents), London. The memoir forms the basis of this chapter but as with any such account (or oral history interview) details can be corroborated via official documents.

ORBs for the squadrons in which Tony served can be viewed in Air 27 at TNA. These are on microfilm, which requires patience especially when looking for a specific event. It is always worth checking to see if such material has been digitised. Additionally, any Internet search engine should throw up basic information on RAF squadrons. Always treat the web with caution as content is unedited. A history of the service can be found at: www.raf.mod.uk/ rafhome.html. At: www.152hyderabad.co.uk there is a service history of No. 152 Squadron, c. 1939–67 and this includes a facsimile of the above ORB together with other features.

Other TNA sources include AIR 29 Miscellaneous Units which contains records for FTSs. These tend to comprise technical reports and numerous photographs that might be of interest from a family history perspective. AIR 32 includes a report on flying training *c.* 1914–45 that has relevance to Tony's later service in Rhodesia.

Ideally, when researching a pilot access to their Flying Log Books will help confirm details such as sorties undertaken, aircraft flown and when and where an individual served. AIR 4 at TNA contains a selection of aircrew's Flying Log Books. Tony's remained within his family but it was possible to appreciate much of his active service via No. 152 Squadron's ORB. Even so, it is worth checking if any documentation, including Flying Log Books, remains within your own family, especially if you are researching a relative who was a pilot.

There are three books that are invaluable in helping to navigate a path through official RAF records: Simon Fowler, Peter Elliot, Roy Conyers Nesbit and Christina Goulter's *RAF Records in the PRO* (PRO Publications, 1994); Phil Tomaselli's *Tracing Your Air Force Ancestors* (Pen & Sword, 2007); and William Spencer's *Air Force Records: A Guide For Family Historians* (TNA, 2009).

John Terraine's *The Right of the Line* (Wordsworth Editions, 1997) discusses the role of the RAF in Europe *c.* 1939–45, including operations in the Mediterranean. Air Chief Marshal Sir Michael Armitage's *The Royal Air Force: An Illustrated History* (Brockhampton Press, 1998) covers the Second World War. Details of British manufactured aircraft deployed by the RAF *c.* 1939–45 are in David Mondey's lavishly illustrated *The Hamlyn Concise Guide to British Aircraft of World War Two* (Chancellor Press, 1995). While Jerry Scutts's *Spitfire in Action* (Squadron/Signal Publications, 1980) provides further information on that famous fighter. Roger A. Freeman's *The Royal Air Force of World War Two in Colour* (Brockhampton Press, 1999) comprises a superb collection of wartime photographs, including shots of Harvards from No. 20 SFS over Rhodesia.

Notes

1. Second World War Experience Centre, Acc. No. LEEW 2006.597, James Anthony Tooth, 'Untitled Memoir', p. 1.
2. Ibid., p. 1.
3. Ibid., p. 4.
4. Ibid.
5. Ibid.
6. Ibid., p. 5.
7. Details of Spitfires can be found in David Mondey's *The Hamlyn Concise Guide to British Aircraft of World War Two* (Chancellor Press, 1995), pp. 197–207.
8. SWEEC, Acc. No. LEEW 2006.597, James Anthony Tooth, 'Untitled Memoir', p. 7.
9. Air Chief Marshal Sir Michael Armitage, *The Royal Air Force: An Illustrated History* (Brockhampton, Press, 1998), p. 166.

10. SWEEC, Acc. No. LEEW 2006.597, James Anthony Tooth, 'Untitled Memoir', p. 8.
11. Ibid., p. 9.
12. Ibid., p. 7.
13. Ibid.
14. Ibid., p. 9.
15. Ibid.
16. Ibid., p. 11.
17. The National Archives, Air 27/1025, No. 152 Squadron ORB, Entry 15/7/43 Ta Kali, Malta.
18. SWEEC, Acc. No. LEEW 2006.597, James Anthony Tooth, 'Untitled Memoir', pp. 14–15.
19. Ibid., p. 17.
20. Ibid.

Chapter 10

A Wren Goes to War –
Jean Gadsden

In 1939 it was decided to re-form the Women's Royal Naval Service (WRNS), better known as the Wrens, that had first operated during 1917–19, before being disbanded. It is important to recognise that although the position of women in society had generally improved by the outbreak of the Second World War, they were still, as one historian noted, 'regarded as inferior to men in almost every kind of work outside the home and family'.[1]

Initially, Wrens were employed solely on administrative or domestic related tasks. So it was perfectly possible for a woman who had say worked in the kitchen in a private house to join up and find herself in the 'galley' at a naval establishment. However, as the war progressed women took on an increasing number of tasks. These ranged from clerical duties to technical ones such as servicing torpedoes and working as air mechanics. The latter proved especially successful as Wrens were able to gain considerable on-the-job experience and perfect their skills at land-based stations. Many Wrens, in fact, proved more adept at the tasks they were given than their male counterparts, albeit they were helped by performing most of them on land rather than under sea-going conditions.

A few Wrens were even given a limited sea-going role, particularly in coastal craft such as motor launches that were not designed to see action. Naval intelligence, including the then top-secret code-breaking work at Bletchley Park, was further dependent on the efforts of several Wrens. Like their comrades in the other branches of the service, they had to endure the hardships of wartime life and work with the constant knowledge that loved ones might be in danger while serving overseas.

By 1944–5 there can have been few naval stations, especially in Britain, that would have felt complete without their complement of Wrens. Around 6,000 also volunteered for overseas postings and were sent as far a field as the Far East and South Africa. Part of the success of the Wrens was down to their wartime director Dame Vera Laughton Mathews, a one time suffragette and woman of drive and energy, who owing to her constant visits to naval establishments was nicknamed 'Tugboat Annie'. She was deeply Christian and 'knew exactly what sort of WRNS she wanted from the start, and fought all the regiments of bureaucrats and civil servants single-handedly to get it right'.[2]

The WRNS could draw upon the rich heritage of the Navy, and particularly that of their First World War predecessors. Most women who joined came from naval families or had friends and/or loved ones already in the service. Recruiting campaigns characterised by posters exhorting women to 'Join the Wrens . . . And Free A Man For The Fleet' were another motivating factor in inspiring women to 'do their bit'. Similarly, the naval uniform was arguably more glamorous and so had greater appeal for many women when compared with the drabber equivalents worn by the ATS and WAAF. The WRNS had a degree of autonomy as the women didn't come under the same regulations as the rest of the Navy. As one wartime Wren explained, this had certain comforting advantages:

> we were able to buy our own underclothes. We used to have coupons and we were allowed so many coupons a year . . . we were also allowed to wear stockings. Instead of having to wear the black wool stockings we were allowed to wear rayon. And then, of course, when nylons came in we were allowed to wear nylons . . . which . . . for most of the time the other two services weren't. And I suppose really it made us feel better because we could please ourselves to a certain extent.[3]

Jean Gadsden was born in July 1922 in Guiseley, near Leeds where her father was a cardboard-box manufacturer. He had served in the RAMC during the First World War before transferring to the Royal Flying Corps. In 1939, shortly before the outbreak of war, he was called up to serve with the RAF. The family was still living in Guiseley at the outbreak of the Second World War when Jean was completing her education.

On her father's recommendation, Jean had opted for a commercial education rather than take up the opportunity of a scholarship at a grammar school. Consequently, she spent three years at Fox's Commercial School in Bradford, before obtaining a secretarial post to the director of one of the Bradford Dyers Association (BDA) branches in Guiseley.

This was classed as a reserved occupation because the BDA, chiefly concerned with textile dying and finishing, was heavily involved in the manufacture of uniforms and items of equipment, particularly canvas belts for the armed forces. However, by 1943 Jean had decided to volunteer for the WRNS and aspired to become a 'writer', the naval designation for all types of clerical or secretarial work. She hoped that this would allow her to maintain her skill at shorthand.

A relative, her fiancé and several of their friends were already in the Navy which provided a further impetus for volunteering for that service. She went to *Mill Hill*, London for initial training and selection for a particular trade.

> After my medical examination I waited on tenterhooks for the 'yes' or 'no' to come from the Admiralty. They accepted me and as I had never been away from home for more than two weeks I was full of trepidation when I made my journey to London with my one obligatory suitcase and reported to a forbidding white building in North London which still seemed to be under construction (we were given later to understand that it was to be the new HQ for the Imperial Cancer Research Laboratories at Mill Hill). Inside, the bare floors, cold undecorated walls, draughty corridors and uninviting atmosphere were as daunting as a penal institution.[4]

Mill Hill was a 'stone frigate', an institution on dry land that operated along the same lines as a commissioned ship in the Navy. As Jean explained, 'we walked on the deck, ate in the mess, cooked in the galley, slept on bunks in cabins, bathroom was ablutions and WCs heads. We went ashore and being late was being adrift.'[5] For new recruits like Jean the environment was a harsh one with more than its fair share of unpleasant tasks such as scrubbing decks, or serving food in the mess. She 'hated the dreadful place and was overwhelmed by home-sickness'.[6]

After her initial training Jean was selected to attend Westfield College, a few miles away, where training for the Navy's communications branch occurred. This entailed preparing women to work in all aspects of communications including as wireless and telephone switchboard operators. She was selected for instruction on the teleprinter, a machine similar to a manual typewriter but which was electrically powered, requiring individuals to 'type slower and to a steady rhythm'.[7]

This lasted a few weeks but then Jean found herself in trouble with the first officer of the WRNS:

> my father's cousin who was the relative in the navy was a commander at the Admiralty and he was debriefing survivors from the ships you see. And I didn't know it was against the rules but I rang him up and I was in the office or and had a word with him. Anyway he said 'well

A wartime portrait of Jean Gadsden proudly wearing her WRNS uniform. (SWWEC)

come down to Admiralty,' and, of course, I got on a, well not a charge exactly but I was reported to the first officer and that was that for me.[8]

Consequently, she was removed from the teleprinter course and transferred to the Signals Distribution Office where she was tasked with general signals work. This was actually a blessing as the last thing Jean really wanted to do was to be stuck, sat behind a teleprinter all day long. Her duties entailed typing out signals that were then distributed to other naval commands or stations, although she herself would not have known where they were to be sent. Occasionally, signals might have been in code but typically they were in plain language. Jean enjoyed it, 'I was very happy . . . because it was a more general sort of atmosphere in the office because you had the people coming in with the signals instead of just sitting in a little cubicle . . . with two or three other teleprinter operators just churning out the signals'.[9]

121

The Wrens were granted an evening pass into London once a week. On one occasion Jean and a friend went to see a film. The 'cinema was crowded, cigarette smoke filled the air and there was an overpowering smell of warm, damp overcoats'.[10] Half-way through the screening a sign flashed up notifying the audience that an air raid was in progress but the film would continue for those wishing to stay. Although less frequent than during the Blitz, air raids were still a threat to London and other cities, and could be a terrifying experience for anyone unlucky enough to be caught up in one.

Jean and her friend faced the dilemma of whether to stay in the 'cinema and risk a direct hit or whether to run for it'.[11] In the event they chose the latter option which proved a fortunate choice.

> The film was running late and we didn't want to be put on a charge for being late so we made our way out of the cinema into the blacked-out street where searchlights were stabbing the sky, ack-ack guns were firing all round, fire engines were racing through the streets and air-raid wardens shouted at us to get under cover as we chased up the road. We arrived back, panic stricken, hats awry, to be greeted by an ashen faced regulating officer . . . 'where on earth have you been; you're adrift and ought to be on a charge. Get a hot drink and go to bed and don't do it again!' We heard later that soon after our visit, the cinema had a direct hit.[12]

After completing her training in London Jean received a posting to Inverness, Scotland, although at the time she had no idea of where she was heading. Together with about twenty other Wrens, she was bundled onto an overcrowded troop train at King's Cross for the long journey northwards under wartime conditions. The small party eventually arrived at Inverness where they were transported in an open truck in the freezing Scottish air to Cameron Barracks, the Regimental HQ of the Queens Own Cameron Highlanders. This had been requisitioned by the Navy as HQ Combined Operations Invasion Force 'S' (Sword).

As Jean noted in her recollections, it was imperative that the forces destined for participation in the 'second front', or Operation Overlord, were as fully prepared as possible, and much training was undertaken in Scotland by all kinds of units:

> Naval crews were being trained in the Cromarty and Moray Firths on how to manoeuvre and beach the ungainly landing craft which were to carry the troops, tanks and all the paraphernalia of war to form the

spearhead of the invasion of Europe. Aircraft recognition was an essential part of this training as was the use of small anti-aircraft Oerlikon guns mounted on the stern of the craft.[13]

She expected to work in the Signals Office but HQ Combined Operations had a full complement of signals ratings. Consequently, Jean was asked if she would assist the gunnery officer in preparing his lectures on the Oerlikon. This was a drum-fed, light anti-aircraft weapon of 20mm calibre, with a rate of fire of 650 rounds per minute and crew of three. It was 'used to give teeth to amphibious landing craft' such as the LCI, or landing craft infantry.[14]

Many of the crews undergoing training were inexperienced both in the use of landing craft and the deployment of these guns. The gunnery officer based his lectures on the relevant training manuals/pamphlets, interspersed with his own notes and slides. Jean's job was to write up his notes into a coherent and manageable form. Sometimes she would attend the lectures herself and even went aboard a landing craft, although never actually sailed in one.

There was very little time off for recreational activities, apart from dances and the occasional trip to the cinema in Inverness. Accommodation was pretty basic:

> no heating of any sort. The cabins or barracks, we called them 'cabins,' of course. There were about fifty of us in, in one of them, and there was a little black iron stove right at the far end and that was it, . . . We had to have the windows open when we went to bed, and sometimes . . . we went to bed in our greatcoats and our hats and gloves and bell bottoms. And in the morning, well, more than once in the morning there would be snow on the bottom of the bunks you know when we wakened up.[15]

Near the end of her time at Cameron Barracks Jean and the rest of the ship's company were reviewed in the freezing cold by the Prime Minster Winston Churchill. They had to be marched constantly around the parade ground while waiting for him, just so they could keep warm. Subsequently, during the spring of 1944 she was transported to the South Coast and then, with a small party of Wrens, sent to Exbury House.

This was part of a beautiful country estate on the edge of the New Forest belonging to the Rothschild family, which had been requisitioned by Combined Operations RN and turned it into HMS *Mastodon*, which performed a significant role in the ongoing preparations for D-Day. Here Jean worked in the Signals Office and was again involved with signals distribution.

Personnel tended to work in three watches so that you might be on duty from 8am until 2pm and then come back on duty from around 6.30pm and work through the night. There was a teleprinter and a switchboard operator, alongside several typists including Jean. All sorts of pre-invasion exercises occurred, particularly of an amphibious nature, and this ensured that there was plenty of traffic for the Signals Office to deal with.

Today it is perhaps difficult to comprehend fully both the atmosphere that existed during the spring/summer of 1944, and the shear scale of the preparations required by Operation Overlord (D-Day). Assets for Operation Neptune, the naval component of D-Day, were drawn largely from the RN. Onshore assembly areas around the New Forest and on the South Coast were, as Jean described:

> saturated with Allied troops, tanks, guns and armaments of all shapes and sizes, trucks large and small for mile after mile in and around the New Forest. Naval ships of all types and sizes crammed into the coastal waters and Solent and we in our signals office sending, receiving and distributing signals to bases, ships and flotilla skippers, while countless naval 'exercises' were being held as dress rehearsals for the real thing.[16]

Leading up to the invasion stringent security measures were enforced with troops being confined to their assembly areas and most other units prevented from communicating with the 'outside world'. As Jean recalled, 'we weren't allowed ashore, we weren't allowed any letters and letters were not allowed out. We'd no communications . . . all the time I was in the WRNS we weren't allowed cameras and we weren't allowed to take photographs'.[17] In the interests of security neither were the Wrens permitted to keep personal diaries.

Jean was on duty in the Signals Office in the basement of Exbury House on 5 June when a momentous event occurred, D-Day was postponed for 24 hours owing to bad weather. She, in fact, had to type a signal for distribution to ships in the Beaulieu River area notifying naval commanders of the delay. This was awful for the troops, who would be involved in the initial assaults, as they had to remain anxiously 'imprisoned' in their cramped landing craft or ships. Similarly, for personnel like Jean who were effectively working 'behind the scenes' the wait was agonising.

Then in the early hours of 6 June the signal came from General Eisenhower that the invasion was to go ahead. Someone, possibly the signals officer or chief petty officer, approached Jean in the Signals Office and said, 'This is it', and gave her 'the signal to type. So it had to be typed to send out to the flotilla leaders in the Beaulieu River.'[18] Shortly before going off watch she and a friend were granted permission to go down to the river and watch the last of the invasion vessels moored there make off for their assembly points in the Solent. She remembered that with the troops gone the base was shrouded in an 'awful deathly silence'.[19]

Jean continued to serve at HMS *Mastodon* until shortly before VE-Day. Largely, her work continued to entail typing out signals so they could be dispatched to the relevant naval commands. In the wake of D-Day information was constantly streaming in relating to the supporting naval operations and there was an urgent need to maintain the logistical system. This all generated signals traffic between naval bases and headquarters units that had to be handled by personnel like Jean.

As in Scotland, Jean did not have much free time, especially prior to D-Day, but when off duty it was sometimes possible to go into Southampton. Here Wrens could enjoy the cinema, dances and even a few shops. The accommodation was a vast improvement on what she had experienced at Cameron Barracks as she and other Wrens were billeted in the servants' quarters at Exbury House. Here, owing to their long work hours in the Signals Office, they were relieved from enduring captain's rounds or routine inspections common to many postings.

As the war progressed the workload at HMS *Mastodon*, which had been heavily involved in D-Day and the resulting naval operations, started to slacken off. At the end of April 1945 Jean was posted to Poole, Dorset, where she was involved in 'paying off the motor torpedo boats from the coastal forces as they were coming back . . . to us for decommissioning'.[20] During the first few years of the war the Navy deployed several types of light craft for operations in coastal waters, particularly the English Channel. However, by 1943 wartime experience had highlighted the need for MTBs and motor gun boats (MGBs) to be 'merged as a single type by the simple expedient of providing the former with greater gun power and adding torpedo tubes to the latter'.[21] These were the sort of craft that Jean was dealing with and she remained at Poole for the rest of the war.

Rather than work solely in signals distribution Jean was now involved in a multitude of duties and really enjoyed it. As she noted, it was 'lovely there. I was teleprinter operator, signals distributor, typing the signals for distribution, receiving the signals, doing shorthand notes and practicing semaphore and having gun practice and all that sort of thing'.[22]

On VE-Day she and other Wrens went into Poole and there were some jollities such as singing the *Lambeth Walk* in the streets. However, on the

Throughout the war the Navy employed a variety of coastal craft to defend British waters. Here a MTB is being put through its paces and it was craft like this that Jean Gadsden was involved in decommissioning towards the end of the war. (SWWEC)

whole people seemed too tired to bother and Jean recalled little in the way of public celebration. Perhaps this is unsurprising given that most people were worn out after enduring years of war, and the war with Japan was still not over.

Jean was demobbed in 1946 but not before she had enjoyed a ride in one of the MTBs she was involved in decommissioning. The sea was rough and the skipper said 'would you like to take over?' So she 'took over and drove round the Solent for about half an hour and then came back'.[23]

After the war she married and settled back in her native Yorkshire. Many years later in 1990 the decision was taken to send women to sea in combatant vessels and in 1994 the WRNS as a separate entity, as Jean knew it, was abolished and fully integrated with the rest of the Navy. When interviewed about her naval service in 2000 Jean was moved to state:

I think they were wonderful years, but they were frightening years, but I think we learned a lot. And I think there was far more communal spirit then than ever there has been since. I think people generally had a sense of fighting for survival that hasn't ever been known since, and I sometimes think when people today keep on saying about 'well it's time to forget the war and time to forget it and let it rest,' I think it shouldn't be forgotten that although since then we've had several extremely unpleasant wars and, and fighting services have been involved and there's been a lot of loss of life I think the Second World War was completely different because this country then was fighting for its very survival.[24]

Researching Jean Gadsden

When researching a Wren's service numerous secondary sources are available that provide helpful background. These include the following general histories: Eileen Bigland's *The Story of the W.R.N.S.* (Nicholson & Watson, 1946); Dame Vera Laughton Mathews's *Blue Tapestry* (Hollis & Carter, 1948); and Ursula Stuart Mason's *The Wrens 1917–1977: a history of the Women's Royal Naval Service* (Educational Explorers Ltd, 1977). Additionally, Admiral Sir Reginald H. S. Bacon (ed.), *Britain's Glorious Navy* (Odhams Press Ltd, c. 1940–5) and Brian Lavery's *Churchill's Navy: The Ships, Men and Organisation 1939–1945* (Conway, 2006) contain useful chapters on the WRNS.

Similarly, a number of published memoirs of wartime Wrens are available and the following provide a guide to this type of material. Lilian Pickering's *The War Years by 'One Small Wren'* (Athena Press, 2006) traces the author's service in Britain and South Africa; Roxane Houston's *Changing Course* (Grub Street, 2005) similarly describes the author's war experiences as a Wren and later an officer, including a posting to HQ SEAC Kandy, Ceylon (Sri Lanka), HMS *Hathi*.

Louisa M. Jenkins's *Bellbottoms and Blackouts: Memories of a Wren* (iUniverse, Inc, 2004) describes the author's service in Britain, including work as a teleprinter operator. While Christian Lamb's *I Only Joined For The Hat: Redoubtable Wrens at War . . . Their Trials, and Triumphs* (Bene Factum Publishing, 2007) is a compilation of several wartime Wren's memories, interlaced with those of the author who was eventually commissioned and involved in the Combined Operations planning for D-Day.

The SWWEC and IWM, London (Department of Documents) hold letters, interviews and other archival material relating to a wide selection of wartime

Wrens. This includes Jean Gadsden, who was interviewed by Pat Clarke on behalf of SWWEC in 2000. Their archive also includes her 'Recollections of the Second World War' and a small selection of scanned photographic images.

TNA are a further source of material relating to Wrens, although much of this is of an administrative or operational as opposed to genealogical nature. Even so, it is worth checking their holdings, especially: ADM 1 Admiralty, and Ministry of Defence, Navy Department Correspondence and Papers; ADM 179 Admiralty, Portsmouth Station: Correspondence; and ADM 199 Admiralty: War History Cases and Papers, Second World War. For example, ADM 1/29523 'Birthday Honours List 1944: Awards to officers of the WRNS' might be useful from a family history perspective. While on D-Day: ADM 179/504 'Operation Neptune Report of proceedings of Force "S" during assault on the coast of Normandy' provides a flavour of the type of official records that can be found to supplement sources dealing with an individual's personal experience.

There are two useful websites at: www.wrens.org.uk, the Association of Wrens site and www.royalnavalmuseum.org/info-sheets-WRNS.htm, the Royal Naval Museum, Portsmouth site, both of which include brief historical background on the service.

The preparations and waiting ahead of D-Day, which Jean and so many other service personnel experienced, are covered by Cornelius Ryan's *The Longest Day* (Wordsworth Editions, 1999), first published in 1959; Harry C. Butcher's *Three Years with 1942–1945* (William Heinemann Ltd, 1946); and General Eisenhower's *Crusade in Europe* (William Heinemann Ltd, 1948).

Notes

1. Brian Lavery, *Churchill's Navy: The Ships, Men and Organisation 1939–1945* (Conway, 2006), p. 153.
2. Christian Lamb, *I Only Joined For The Hat: Redoubtable Wrens at War . . . Their Trials, and Triumphs* (Bene Factum Publishing, 2007), pp. 15–16.
3. Second World War Experience Centre, Acc. No. 2000.708, transcript of tape 635, Mrs J. Gadsden interviewed by Pat Clarke, 26 September 2000, pp. 6–7.
4. SWWEC, Acc. No. LEEWW:2000.708.1, 'Recollections of the Second World War' by Jean Gadsden, compiled *c.* 2000, p. 1.
5. Ibid.
6. Ibid.
7. Louisa M. Jenkins, *Bellbottoms and Blackouts: Memories of a Wren* (iUniverse, Inc, 2004), pp. 2–3.
8. SWWEC, Acc. No. 2000.708, transcript of tape 635, Mrs J. Gadsden interviewed by Pat Clarke, 26 September 2000, p. 3.
9. Ibid., p. 4.
10. SWWEC, Acc. No. LEEWW:2000.708.1, 'Recollections of the Second World War' by Jean Gadsden, compiled *c.* 2000, p. 2.
11. Ibid.

12. Ibid.
13. Ibid.
14. Ian V. Hogg and John Bachelor, *Weapons and War Machines* (Phoebus Publishing Co., 1976), p. 143.
15. SWWEC, Acc. No. 2000.708, transcript of tape 635, Mrs J. Gadsden interviewed by Pat Clarke, 26 September 2000, p. 6.
16. SWWEC, Acc. No. LEEWW:2000.708.1, 'Recollections of the Second World War' by Jean Gadsden, compiled *c*. 2000, p. 3.
17. SWWEC, Acc. No. 2000.708, transcript of tape 635, Mrs J. Gadsden interviewed by Pat Clarke, 26 September 2000, p. 9.
18. Ibid., p. 10.
19. SWWEC, Acc. No. LEEWW:2000.708.1, 'Recollections of the Second World War' by Jean Gadsden, compiled *c*. 2000, p. 3.
20. SWWEC, Acc. No. 2000.708, transcript of tape 635, Mrs J. Gadsden interviewed by Pat Clarke, 26 September 2000, p. 13.
21. H. T. Lenton and J. J. Colledge, *Warships of World War II* (Ian Allan Ltd, 1980), p. 544.
22. SWWEC, Acc. No. 2000.708, transcript of tape 635, Mrs J. Gadsden interviewed by Pat Clarke, 26 September 2000, p. 13.
23. Ibid., p. 16.
24. Ibid.

Chapter 11

A Signalman in the Far East –
Brian W. Aldiss

The Royal Corps of Signals were formed in 1920 from the Signals Service of the Corps of Royal Engineers. During the Second World War it was responsible for Army communications down to regimental headquarters' level or the equivalent, a task that routinely involved the deployment of radio, wire, teleprinter or telegraph signalling equipment.

The Corps performed an invaluable function in all theatres, including the Far East, where 'in the jungle areas, . . . wireless equipment was badly blanketed by the foliage, and at least initially, was not tropicalized resulting in fungus and deterioration in insulation'.[1] Additionally, movement was hampered by the underdeveloped jungle terrain and operations tended to be launched with a shortage of both supplies and personnel. Often,'fighting was conducted by relatively small columns, with open flanks, widely dispersed, and frequently with no line of supply other than by air'.[2]

Service in the Far East brought with it the threat of death not only from enemy action but from tropical diseases. Signallers had to be prepared to adapt, improvise and learn on the job. By August 1945 over 4,000 signalmen had died during the Burma Campaign as they attempted to keep communications functioning under these trying conditions.

Brian Aldiss was born in East Dereham, Norfolk in August 1925. His father ran the men's outfitters in a family owned and run department store. He attended a preparatory school on the coast at Bacton and recalled that it was a'ludicrous shambling'establishment.[3] From there he was sent to Framlingham College, Suffolk, which he despised. When war was declared he was 'saved' by his father's decision to move from the Norfolk coast to Devon in the belief that it was safer there. The family ended up straying over the border into Cornwall and stayed near Bude. Here Brian stood outdoors with his father in September 1939 and'listened to a radio coming from a caravan, and the radio solemnly declared that from that moment on Great Britain was at war with Germany'.[4]

Subsequently, he was dispatched to a public school on the edge of Exmoor where he was far happier than he had been at Framlingham. In particular, he remembered that its isolated location coupled with the outbreak of war fostered a strong sense of camaraderie among the masters and the boys. Initially, 'one's understanding was rather poor and war just seemed to be a permanent condition. It was something that as far as one knew it would go on for ever.'[5] However, once he became a sixth-former two distinct concerns arose, 'fear that at any moment you would be called-up and you would have to go and fight and you would be sucked into this maelstrom. But there was the other fear that if you weren't careful it might all be over and you would miss it – the biggest initiation rite in history.'[6]

In August 1943, shortly after his eighteenth birthday, Brian volunteered to join the Army. He was issued with a rail pass and travel money so that he could take a train from Devon to Britannia Barracks, Norwich. The barracks were traditionally home to the Royal Norfolk Regiment and were built on a hill dominating that city. Ironically, it was there that his father had been called-up during the First World War.

Brian had briefly served in the Home Guard and at his school there was an OTC, both of which helped him cope with the shock of basic training. He recalled, 'I went in uniform and felt that was a great advantage . . . whereas most of the other wretches called-up were in civilian clothes and quite lost, . . . it was never any difficulty to be in the army after ten years at boarding school'.[7]

After basic training he was posted to Catterick, North Yorkshire to join the Royal Corps of Signals as a comparatively lowly trainee signalman. Signals training at Catterick was expanded to meet the urgent demands of wartime and by 1943 it was regularly handling over 4,000 students simultaneously, something that required new accommodation to be built. Brian became particularly efficient at working in Morse code and was able to transmit and receive eighty words per minute.

Brian was interviewed with regard to being posted to an Officer Cadet Training Unit. His public-school background would have been an asset, particularly from his superior's perspective, but as he himself admitted he proved unable to deliver orders effectively. Consequently, he was destined to see out his war service in the ranks where he kept his educational background a secret. However, he enjoyed the coarseness of the soldierly humour, diversity of language and regional accents that he encountered.

We had one fellow in our squad who was into the 'thee' and 'thou'. Still extraordinary primitive residue of language, who would say 'thy cans't do summat or other' you know, and very odd. And at one time he was stuttering away and a Cockney said to him 'tha cans't speak as well as coulds't cans't' . . . so there was a lot of this sort of mickey-taking, but I think that on the whole it was very good humoured.[8]

After completing his signal training Brian was deemed too young for an immediate posting on active service. This perturbed him as he had lost touch with those mates with whom he had joined up. While they went on overseas postings, he was still stuck in Britain faced with the prospect of further training. Eventually, he was allowed to go on an overseas draft and arrived in Bombay during the late summer of 1944.

Brian was posted as a reinforcement to 2nd British Division, a formation that saw extensive service in India and Burma and whose distinctive insignia comprised two white crossed keys on a black square. The division were part of Fourteenth Army, sometimes dubbed the 'Forgotten Army', that had been established during late 1943 to conduct operations in Burma.

Initially, acclimatisation and further signals training took place in India before Brian was posted to Burma. By now the Japanese 15th Army had been pushed back to the line of the Chindwin having suffered at least 60,000 casualties. The British maintained a presence in the Arakan and hoped to renew the fight once the monsoon ended in December. Brian was acutely aware that places such as Kohima and Imphal, where intense battles had been fought, had assumed a near legendary status among troops in the Far East. Although he missed these encounters, he did come under fire during his service in theatre and witnessed death first-hand, particularly of enemy troops.

As a signalman Brian's primary function was to provide divisional communications using a fullerphone, a piece of technology dating from the First World War. It was a 'miserable little thing . . . black . . . about eighteen inches long, worked by batteries, which you had to test by licking your fingers and putting them across the terminals and we were always very, very squeamish about that. It had a key, and . . . earphones so that you could transmit and receive in Morse'.[9] Additionally, he would sometimes accompany a linesman in a truck laying out cables that would then be connected so as to pick up a signal.

As the war progressed he became involved in the advance towards Mandalay and Rangoon. However, as a signaller he was never at the forefront of the action. Rather, his signal office followed up in the wake of combat units and acted as an intermediary ensuring that adequate communications were maintained between the forward brigades and divisional HQ. This enabled

A highly evocative scene showing British troops advancing past the war-ravaged remains of Burmese buildings. (Taylor Library)

orders and reports to be both received and transmitted as efficiently and speedily as possible.

Recalling the type of 'daily' routine he experienced in Burma, Brian noted:

We knew all the brigades and the traffic was very continuous and those fuller phones were manned twenty four hours a day. We had three shifts. S-Relief was divided into three shifts. The first shift would go bright and breezy at eight in the morning and would work until one o'clock and then they would have the afternoon off. This was ideally. In actual fact when we were in action the system broke down. But then you would have the afternoon off, which is to say you would be doing something else, and then in the evening you would go on at six o'clock and would work through the night until eight next morning. So there were sort of three divisions of the day. The difficulty about this was with regards to eating because you would turn up late at the improvised mess ... and there would be nothing left or it would be cold and there was very scummy water to wash your utensils in ... most of the time you were tired because ... the night you were meant to be sleeping you might be on guard.[10]

The first Japanese Brian saw was hardly an imposing or frightening figure. He was virtually naked and'had very tattered shorts and some sort of thing tied round his tummy. No boots, and he was running looking quite cheerful with a British squaddie behind him with a fixed bayonet sort of prodding him.'[11]

However, the enemy was not always so benign and would mount desperate rearguard actions in the face of the British advance. Bunkers offered stubborn resistance while Japanese snipers who effectively embarked on suicide missions were another bugbear. Brian encountered one of the latter early on during his operational service while 2nd Division was massing for an attack at Yzagio. An enemy sniper was holed up in a white stone pagoda near to where he and other troops were parading. Suddenly, a shot rang out and one of their officers fell down dead. The sniper was only neutralised when a mortar was deployed to shoot the top off of the pagoda.

Episodes like this demonstrated that no one, not even signalmen 'behind the lines', was safe from a tenacious enemy such as the Japanese. On another occasion while establishing a new site for the signal office Brian was confronted by piles of dead being cleared by the Pioneer Corps. These were either Japanese or possibly Koreans who had been conscripted by the enemy.

All the bodies had been blown up and turned black and had coalesced into a sort of solid wall with their feet sticking out and their heads sticking out ... and it was a most extraordinary sight and absolutely buzzing with bluebottles, and I thought 'well this is the real thing'. Although I was shocked I kind of welcomed the shock. I can't describe it but there was a sort of exultation in seeing, as it were, the worst, the worst that you can possibly find. It was there.[12]

By contrast, during the campaign he also encountered the Naga people who went about their daily business despite the war and were principally concerned with tea planting.

It was curious in the middle of this war where we could look across to a bit of wild country where we were told Japanese snipers might be loitering, and there were these rather handsome looking people shinning up and down through thousands of feet every day to gather tea. I thought it wonderful to be there – inspiring.[13]

British infantry engaged in jungle fighting in the sort of awkward and rugged terrain that would have been familiar to Brian Aldiss. The rifleman is armed with a .303 Lee–Enfield with fixed bayonet, while the lead soldier appears to be armed with a sub-machine gun or carbine. (Taylor Library)

Initially, he was very aware that he had to earn his place in S-Section as he had yet to 'get his knees brown' like the hardened signalmen and NCOs that he was serving alongside. On reflection, Brian reckoned he was accepted owing to his cheerful demeanour and good sense of humour, valuable attributes when stuck out in the middle of the jungle.

Relationships between junior and more senior ranks tended to be good because they were on active service overseas so there was none of the 'bull' that would accompany British postings, notably an absence of drill and saluting. He fondly remembers one sergeant confiding in him, 'oh what misery this is. I wish I were in bed with some low down woman in Skegness.'[14] Later such experiences would influence his post-war writing, particularly *A Soldier Erect* which traces the sexual escapades of men from the fictional Royal Mendip Borderers as they are plunged into the war in the Far East.

Another feature of life during the Burma Campaign was that men could become 'jungley' or adopt a wild manner that complemented being in such a rugged and awkward theatre. An extension of this was to become a 'puggle wallah', a term adopted from Urdu and applied to troops who had gone a step beyond 'jungley'. In Brian's unit, for example, there was a kindly orderly who coped with the isolation and tough conditions by drilling alone at night with his rifle and giving himself orders.

Brian discovered that it was an education being surrounded by troops who lacked his comparatively comfortable upbringing. After the war he realised that for many men their less well-off backgrounds were in fact an asset under active service conditions and helped them cope. As he explained, it provided them with a form of 'physiological protection' and 'if something went wrong they would say "well, what do you expect?"'[15] In other words, they expected little from life and so were not overawed by the rough conditions experienced in the Army at that time.

As the Japanese retreated to Rangoon, Brian starting training for Operation Zipper, Lord Mountbatten's plan to capture Port Swettenham on the north-west coast of Malaya and precipitate a southward advance on Singapore. This was scheduled for October 1945 and would have been a tough proposition, not least due to the stubbornness of the Japanese defenders. However, the dropping of the two atomic bombs and surrender of Japan spared Brian's unit from becoming involved in what might have been a costly operation.

Brian was comparatively low down on the list for demobilisation, especially as he was serving alongside soldiers who had been in the Far East much longer than he had. This tended to breed resentment against Britain and as he put it, 'we had been shipped out there and no one had any idea when we were going to get back'.[16] Likewise, as he was under 21 he was too young to vote in the 1945 general election which increased his bitterness. He was old enough to fight for his country but not to have a say on who governed it.

After VJ-Day Brian was posted to Bombay (Mumbai) and re-mustered as a wireless operator in 26th Indian Division. Soon he was dispatched to Sumatra as Indonesian separatists tried to seize independence from the Dutch in the wake of the Japanese surrender. His division was part of the forces being used primarily to re-instate Dutch rule, repatriate former POWs and return Japanese troops to their homeland.

As it transpired, British and other units had to rely on their more numerous former enemies to help 'police' the Dutch East Indies (Indonesia). This created some unusual situations:

picture a restaurant in Pedang, quite a pleasant little restaurant, and sitting at one table am I with my British mates . . . and we are armed with Sten guns [a sub-machine gun of 9mm calibre]. At the next table there are the Indians. They are armed with rifles. They are sitting there chatting away. At another table there were four Dutch. They had got carbines and revolvers. They were sitting there. At another table there were four Japs and they were sitting there with their carbines and are all eating ice cream or something, all talking minding our own business, . . . being served by the Chinese . . . the only currency that was acceptable to all sides was forged Japanese notes which had absolutely no value because . . . Japan had gone . . . but they were paper that everyone acknowledged so they were acceptable.[17]

Brian returned to Britain in July 1947 and immediately missed the warm climate and vibrant, colourful life he had experienced in Sumatra. By comparison, post-war Britain appeared cold, shabby and extremely dull. People were trying to recover from the war and spared little interest for yet another serviceman who had just been demobbed.

As an aspiring writer, he obtained a job in a bookshop in Oxford. Eventually, writing would allow him to offload many of the experiences and emotions that were bound up with his Army service in the Far East. As he explained, his service had both a positive and negative effect on him. On the one hand, it robbed him of his youth but on the other it brought him into contact with 'people of all shades of opinion and all ways of life . . . I had lived behind the privet hedges of my middle class upbringing and then was exposed to the full blasts of under-privileged England'.[18]

Since the 1950s Brian has established himself as an award-winning author, particularly of science fiction and was awarded the OBE. For many years he also worked as a book seller and literary editor of the *Oxford Mail*. Some of his works reflect his experience in the Far East during the 1940s, notably *The Interpreter* (Interpreter Digit, 1960), which as a central theme has the tangled relationship between imperialists and their subject races. While the last two novels in the Horatio Stubbs saga draw heavily upon his Army service, particularly in their use of language and the characters and images they conjurer up.

Researching Brian W. Aldiss

Brian Aldiss's autobiography *The Twinkling of an Eye: My life as an Englishman* was published by Little, Brown during the mid-1990s and beautifully encapsulates his experiences in Burma with its evocative descriptions of life as a comparatively lowly signalman. By contrast, *Bury My Heart at WH Smith's – A Writing Life* (Coronet Books, 1990) discusses publishing and includes a chapter contextualising the Horatio Stubbs novels. As intimated above, *A Soldier Erect* (Corgi Books, 1971) and *A Rude Awakening* (Weidenfeld & Nicolson, 1978) were heavily inspired by his service in the Far East *c*. 1944–7. Both revolve around the sexual exploits of Horatio Stubbs and his Army mates as they experience service as infantrymen first during the Burma Campaign and subsequently in post-war Sumatra. They are very much a view of 'life from the ranks' in which ordinary soldiers encounter not only the threat of the Japanese enemy but also the frustrations caused by sexual deprivation.

In October 1999 Brian was interviewed by Dr Peter Liddle on behalf of the SWWEC and a copy of the transcripts are available in the archives there. These provide some rich memories of his time in the Far East, although as is often the case with oral history they are vague on dates. However, this need not necessarily be a problem as it is possible to corroborate such details by consulting official documents such as War Diaries or in this case using personal letters. If you are eligible, you may be able to look at an individual's Service Record which would also confirm this type of detail.

Additionally, SWWEC holds hundreds of letters written by Brian to his parents that cover his Army service between 1943 and 1947. He was an avid correspondent, even managing to scrawl a few lines while waiting in the NAAFI queue at Catterick or when on exercise. Later, he wrote home extensively from the Far East and these letters provide further vivid descriptions of the conditions he experienced out there. These are just the type of items that may survive within many other families in Britain and can be used to form an outline of a relative's war service.

Records covering 2nd British Division Signals in the Far East at TNA can be found in WO 172 SEAC War Diaries India, Burma and Malaya. While WO 32 General Series and WO 244 Directorate of Signals: Papers contain several records dealing with the wartime Royal Corps of Signals, including material on training.

William Spencer's *The National Archives Army Records A Guide for Family Historians* (TNA, 2008) and Simon Fowler's *Tracing Your Army Ancestors* (Pen & Sword, 2009) are helpful when researching any wartime soldier, including those that served in the Royal Corps of Signals.

The Royal Signals Museum at Blandford Camp, Dorset traces the history of Army signalling. Additionally, it houses a library and archive and these can be consulted by the public via appointment. Please note the museum does not hold service papers for individual officers and soldiers. Neither does it possess the resources to deal with research enquiries over the telephone. For up-to-date information please visit their website at: www.royalsignals museum.com.

Lieutenant Colonel George Forty's *British Army Handbook 1939–1945* (Sutton Publishing, 2002) is a useful reference tool on the wartime military and includes sections on signal training and equipment. Major General R. F. H. Nalder CB, OBE, *The History of British Army Signals in the Second World War* (Royal Signals Institution, 1953) is the official wartime history of the Corps. Nalder also compiled *The Royal Corps of Signals: A History of its Antecedents and Development circa 1800–1955* (Gale & Polden, 1958) which incorporates chapters on the war in the Far East. Such tomes can be found at the Corps museum archives or second-hand bookshops specialising in military history.

Louis Allen's *Burma The Longest War 1941–45* (Guild Publishing, 1984) is an authoritative account of the campaign. Allen served as a Japanese-speaking intelligence officer in SEAC and brings his personal insight and experience to bear. Field Marshal Viscount Slim's *Defeat into Victory* (Cassell & Co. Ltd, 1956) is a classic work of military history and a moving narrative of the war against the Japanese by the commander of 14th Army. By contrast, George MacDonald Fraser's *Quartered Safe Out Here* (HarperCollins, 2000) is an absorbing and colourful memoir about an ordinary soldier's war in Burma with an infantry battalion. While Major General Julian Thompson's *Forgotten Voices of Burma: The Second World War's Forgotten Conflict* (Ebury Press, 2010) is an oral history of the campaign relying heavily on personal testimony from veterans within the IWM archive.

Notes

1. Lieutenant Colonel George Forty, *British Army Handbook 1939–1945* (Sutton Publishing, 2002), p. 86.
2. Major General R. F. H. Nalder CB, OBE, *The Royal Corps of Signals: A History of its Antecedents and Development circa 1800–1955* (Gale & Polden, 1958), p. 465.
3. Second World War Experience Centre, Acc. No. LEEWW 2005-2812, interview with Mr Brian W. Aldiss by Dr Peter Liddle, October 1999, tape 360, p. 1.
4. Ibid., p. 2.
5. Ibid., p. 3.
6. Ibid.
7. Ibid., p. 4.
8. Ibid., p. 5.
9. SWWEC, Acc. No. LEEWW 2005-2812, interview with Mr Brian W. Aldiss by Dr Peter Liddle, October 1999, tape 361, p. 2.

10. Ibid., p. 3.
11. Ibid., p. 5.
12. Ibid., p. 6.
13. Ibid., p. 1.
14. Ibid., pp. 3–4.
15. Ibid., p. 5.
16. SWWEC, Acc. No. LEEWW 2005-2812, interview with Mr Brian W. Aldiss by Dr Peter Liddle, October 1999, tape 360, p. 6.
17. SWWEC, Acc. No. LEEWW 2005-2812, interview with Mr Brian W. Aldiss by Dr Peter Liddle, October 1999, tape 361, pp. 7–8.
18. Ibid., p. 9.

Chapter 12

A 'Hostilities Only Sailor' with the Royal Navy – Colin Kitching

olin Kitching was born in 1920 in Malaya where his father worked for the Colonial Service as a surveyor. When he was 8 he was sent back to Britain to pursue his education, first at a preparatory school and then at Sedburgh. While the latter was tough, he enjoyed it and proved a competent cross-country runner. Although he was small in stature, especially when he first went to the school, he also managed to play successfully for his house rugby team and enjoyed cricket.

On leaving Sedburgh he went up to Oxford to read Modern History at Hartford College in the late 1930s. With war on the horizon he determined to join the Navy as by his own admission he had not relished his experience of military exercises with his school OTC. As he put it, 'if I was going to die for my country I would rather do it in comfortable circumstances with three square meals a day, board and accommodation, showers, a decent lavatory and so on'.[1]

Having obtained his degree, via the specially shortened curriculum that Oxford introduced in wartime, Colin volunteered for the Navy. He was called up in late December 1940 and sent to HMS *Raleigh* near Plymouth. This had been planned prior to the war but had only recently opened as a basic training establishment. His experience at Sedburgh helped him cope with the 'shock' of basic training as he and other young men from a diverse range of backgrounds were moulded into an effective, disciplined body, primarily via intensive drill.

Afterwards Colin was posted to Devonport Barracks to await drafting to a ship. He was part of a draft to HMS *Edinburgh* then based at Scapa Flow as part of the Home Fleet. She was an improved Southampton or Edinburgh class cruiser that had been built in Newcastle upon Tyne during the late 1930s.

141

Eventually, she was scuttled in the Barents Sea after being torpedoed during May 1942. She was a comparatively large ship with a displacement of 10,000 tons, 850-man crew and top speed of 32 knots.[2]

On joining HMS *Edinburgh* he recalled that wartime volunteers like himself were a source of curiosity to the professional sailors that made up most of the crew.

> I was a total nobody. I knew practically nothing. I mean the basic training was just to get you disciplined and march properly and not look scruffy and so on, and you were taught a bit about knots and all that, but there was so much to learn and I was, well, the six months spent on board Edinburgh were the most remarkable . . . experience of my life . . . The professionalism of the whole thing was unbelievable and I was so impressed with, and I was so taken with the way I was treated, and the rest of the draft. They regarded us as strange beings who knew absolutely nothing, which was true, and we had the mickey taken out of us, but they weren't cruel and they weren't horrible. They just regarded us as slightly half-witted young men who had to be taken in hand and make sure that we didn't let the side down by doing something stupid when it mattered.[3]

Colin was a Commissioned Warranted Candidate, in other words someone who had been identified for future training as an officer. Consequently, he was regularly inspected by his divisional officer. However, as an ordinary seaman and later an able seaman his primary job was to serve as a communications number and fuse setter in one of *Edinburgh*'s twin 4in gun mountings. He recalled his action station inside the revolving mounting as follows:

> seated on a stool . . . with a microphone in one hand communicating with the four inch director top above the bridge, and in front of me a little handle. The shell would be put in with the fuse pushed into an aperture, and I would have a dial and the director top would say what the range fuse had to be set, or to what range the fuse had to be set. I would lower my handle and the pointer on my thing had to meet the pointer which the director top had set. So then that fused the shell.[4]

Additionally, Colin was expected to contribute to the overall running of the ship which would provide him with experience prior to undertaking officer training. Work included conducting routine watches, normally 4 hours on and 4 hours off while at sea, and assisting the general mess party. The latter was

Ordinary Seaman Colin Kitching at his action station aboard HMS Edinburgh.
(SWWEC)

tasked with manhandling food supplies from the storerooms to the galley,
including hundredweight sacks of flour. This involved a difficult route up a
series of ladders and on his first attempt Colin fell over. However, by the time
he left the ship in October 1941 he 'was stronger and fitter than I think I have
ever been since'.[5]

While with *Edinburgh* Colin experienced his first taste of action at sea
during Operation EB, an attempt to seize coding tables for the Enigma
machine known to be aboard German weather-reporting ships stationed in

Arctic waters. Staff at Bletchley Park already had an Enigma machine but with the captured coding tables they would be able to read the enemy's naval cipher system almost instantaneously.

Together with two other cruisers and four destroyers, *Edinburgh* was tasked with targeting the German ship *Munchen* on 7 May 1941. Colin formed part of the boarding party from *Edinburgh* and was escorted by a 'mysterious civilian' who was in fact an officer from naval intelligence. The German captain had thrown his Enigma machine together with the coding tables for May overboard, but inadvertently left those for June in his desk and these were eagerly seized by the British.

> For the first time in my life I was equipped with a revolver and we (the boarding party) were under orders to fight our way on board the *Munchen* if necessary. But the *Somali* [one of the accompanying destroyers] was alongside and most of the *Munchen*'s crew had quickly abandoned ship, leaving – as I remember it – only the captain, another officer and a couple of ratings to receive us, which they did with great courtesy. Indeed one of them kindly helped me over the guardrail. The boarding party had to search the *Munchen* in case the Germans had laid scuttling charges in the bowels of the vessel. In carrying out this duty I was somewhat handicapped by the fact that I didn't know what a scuttling charge looked like. As it happened, there were none and *Edinburgh*'s prize crew sailed the *Munchen* back to Scapa Flow.[6]

Shortly after *Edinburgh* was dispatched to the South Atlantic to intercept a German blockade runner, *The Lech*, but with *Bismarck* at large she was swiftly re-assigned to partake in the hunt of that ship. In steaming up from the South Atlantic she became extremely low on fuel, just when the range between her and *Bismarck* was closing and had to break off the chase to refuel at Londonderry.

Subsequently, in July Colin was to see action again as his ship served as escort during Operation Substance, a relief convoy from Britain to Malta via Gibraltar. It was Colin's first experience of coming under hostile fire. He recalled one savage attack that 'started about eight in the morning and went on certainly till eight at night intermittently. So it was a very long gruelling day. . . . in all I was at my action station for eighteen hours on that day with only the odd break to, putting it bluntly, to go and have a pee.'[7]

Over the next few months Colin continued to experience service aboard *Edinburgh* as she was employed on a variety of convoy escort duties, particularly in the Mediterranean and Atlantic. On leaving the ship he was stationed at HMS *King Alfred* in Hove to undertake his officer training and eventually commissioned as a sub-lieutenant in the RNVR.

In March 1942 he was posted to 4th LCP (L) Flotilla at Inveraray where he assisted in the training of troops in amphibious landing operations on Loch Fine. The LCP (L) were landing craft personnel (large), originally known as 'R-boats'. These were 'a modification of a standard motor boat built by Higgins of New Orleans. They were only lightly armoured, with three quarter inch transverse bulkheads, but fast and could be driven ashore at speed so that no special disembarking arrangements were provided, the troops simply jumping off from the bows onto the beach.'[8]

LCPs of Colin Kitching's flotilla on exercise in the Solent. They were termed 'large' because an even smaller version existed. However, the comparatively small size and frail nature of these plywood craft is clearly evident in this wartime photograph. (SWWEC)

These craft were reputed to have been designed for smuggling alcohol into the USA during the prohibition period. Despite their apparently frail nature, they were fast and eminently seaworthy. However, they were ill-suited to the task that was soon to befall them as Colin's flotilla prepared for Operation Jubilee, the British and Canadian assault on Dieppe (18/19 August 1942).

This was a combined operation in which naval forces, including the 'R-boats', played a significant role. One of the primary objectives was to evaluate the German defensive organisation by mounting what Churchill termed a 'reconnaissance in force'. In turn this would enable the Allies to 'exercise' battle-ready troops already stationed in Britain awaiting the 'second front' and test amphibious warfare techniques and weaponry that might be employed in any full-scale cross-Channel invasion.

Ultimately, Jubilee ended in disaster and the raid cost the Allies over 4,000 men, with the Canadian assault troops suffering the most grievous losses. It was, as one writer put it, a 'tragic failure' owing largely to 'the inflexibility of its plan and its reliance on tactical surprise over a wide area. The fire-power provided in support against coastal defences was absurdly inadequate.'[9] Lessons were learned the hard way, not least of which was the impracticability of capturing a heavily defended port, and these would eventually contribute towards the success of D-Day in 1944.

In early August 1942 4th LCP (L) Flotilla were suddenly moved to HMS *Tormentor*, a naval station on the River Hamble off the Solent, which was the home of the 'R-boats'. Naval officers, including Colin, were briefed that together with 5th LCP (L) Flotilla they were to carry the floating reserve, Les Fusiliers Mont Royal, during Jubilee. These French Canadian troops would be deployed where they were most required rather than being designated a specific beach.

Colin remembered starting the operation in the unusually calm waters of the English Channel. This was a relief as there were 'about twenty-six men on board each boat cramped down in the space around the engine and, if it had been rough, these men would have been terribly ill and in no fit condition the next morning to storm ashore.'[10]

The operation commenced during the early morning and initially the reserve force hung back wondering what was happening. Fortunately, the 'R-boats' presented small targets given the heavy amount of shelling and bombing occurring in the area around Dieppe. Even though the enemy had not been subdued, the decision was made to reinforce White and Red Beach in the centre of the assault area where some of the stiffest resistance had been encountered.

> At seven o'clock we set off in two columns line ahead. This involved getting into a line abreast situation. Twenty-six boats in line abreast, which we had rehearsed in the Solent in the previous week . . . Under heavy fire we carried out this manoeuvre to perfection, and from two

columns in line ahead, we formed one line abreast . . . all heading for the beach.

. . . We all broke through this huge pall of smoke and found ourselves about 200 yards from the central shingle beach at Dieppe with all hell breaking loose and a tremendous din of fire. The hotels at the back of the promenade all had machine gunners firing at us. Fortunately the beach was a sloping one so the closer we got to the beach the less troubled we were by machine gun fire. But . . . by that time they were firing mortar bombs at us.[11]

Colin had taken over the wheel from his coxswain as they sped towards the beach when 'a mortar shell exploded to port and a fragment flew up, cut through my wristwatch strap . . . went across the back of my hand, cut me open in two places very mildly and embedded itself in the wooden instrument panel'.[12]

At Collin's section of the beach the 'R-boats' landed successfully allowing their soldiers to jump off. However, their lieutenant 'crumpled up no more than a dozen strides away' and the general scene was appalling with 'a couple of LCTs . . . lying broadside, burning fiercely. Tanks were stranded on the shingle motionless. Dead and wounded Canadians [from the initial assault] lay everywhere.'[13]

Colin was relieved to extricate his boat from the carnage on the beach but appreciated that picking men up later would prove an even more hazardous operation, particularly as the LCP (L) had no ramp. They kept on the move aware that 'a direct shell hit on a flimsy LCP loaded with high octane petrol resulted in the boat being blown apart'.[14]

At approximately 10am the flotilla was ordered to form up again in an effort to rescue soldiers from the beach. However, it was wisely decided to send in armoured landing craft for this purpose instead. Among other things, Dieppe had demonstrated that the LCP (L) was unsuitable for an opposed landing. As Colin stated, 'nonsense to send a wooden boat into the kind of situation we ran into there'.[15] Consequently, they were converted for other tasks, including smoke laying using a tank of chloro-sulphonic acid. This was pumped out under pressure along a pipe so that when it came into contact with air a dense white cloud of smoke was created. Crews needed to be exceptionally careful to release it with the wind astern so as to avoid any risk of the acidic smoke being blown back onto them.

While Colin and his comrades adjusted to their new role, re-organisations occurred and ultimately his flotilla became part of 702 LCP (L) Flotilla. A year

A view of Red and White Beaches at Dieppe where the 4th and 5th LCP Flotillas landed French Canadian troops on 19 August 1942. It clearly shows the level of destruction in the immediate aftermath of the raid, including a knocked out Churchill tank. (SWWEC)

after Dieppe he was to see action again as part of Operation Starkey, a large-scale feint against Boulogne intended to induce the Germans into believing an invasion was imminent. Ultimately, it achieved very little and failed to convince the enemy that they were under any serious threat.[16] Recollecting Starkey, he noted that:

> we escorted the minesweepers down the Channel, past Calais, and further on than Boulogne. They were in all their majesty . . . looking as if they were sweeping mines. They were shelled by big guns that the Germans had on the coast and we covered them with huge smoke screens to prevent them being hit, and it was quite dodgy from our point of view as well because, some of these shells, although maybe not aimed at us, of course, would in fact fall among us. So that was a very tiring operation because it went on from quite early in the morning . . . I don't think that for a moment the Germans were deceived . . . I remember vividly on a beautiful late afternoon in the Channel about two miles off Boulogne, I looked through my naval binoculars at the sea front . . . there was a cinema, and I could see people queuing for the next showing.[17]

By now Colin was first lieutenant of a flotilla of twelve boats and after being diverted by Starkey he was subsequently to prepare for D-Day. This entailed extensive exercises in the West Country as 702 LCP (L) Flotilla were to form part of Force J, the naval element supporting Juno Beach, and was specifically tasked with escorting landing craft transporting amphibious or Duplex-Drive tanks. Once off Juno Beach the LCPs were to provide smoke-screen cover for these tanks and some of the larger warships operating in that area.

The flotilla left Calshot on the Solent on 5 June 1944 in high spirits knowing that they were about to embark on the operation for which they had spent several months training. 'Soldiers crowded the rails of their troop transports and gave us, in our tiny craft, volleys of cheers. All these years later I am still touched when I think of it.'[18]

Of all the vessels involved in D-Day the LCPs were the smallest to sail to France under their own power. In a force 5 wind this was a significant achievement, particularly as their speed had to be adjusted to keep pace with the slowest of the landing craft they were to escort. Ironically, once at Juno Beach they were not in fact required to produce much smoke as in the rough seas it was decided to take the LCTs straight onto the beach to offload their valuable cargo rather than risk launching the Duplex-Drive tanks at sea. However, those craft not covering the LCTs did support the warships involved in the bombardment.

At around 11am on D-Day the flotilla was sent over to Sword Beach as trouble was expected there given its proximity to the Germans on the eastern flank of the bridgehead. 'Reinforcement and supply operations on that beach would be hazardous and the anchorage at risk: maximum smoke protection would be needed.'[19]

For several weeks after D-Day Colin and the LCP (L) crews were required to lay smoke screens, largely at night when the threat of enemy air action was greatest and because by day it might have confused Allied naval forces more than the enemy, given the amount of shipping operating off Normandy. It was exhausting and stressful work:

> every night we covered the anchorage with smoke . . . running up and down, depending on which direction the wind was coming from, making smoke in the pitch darkness, not knowing whether at any moment an E-boat might turn up. If it had we would have had no chance at all of course. We had a Lewis gun [an air-cooled, drum-fed machine gun of .303 calibre] mounted in the stern, but that would not have coped with an E-boat.[20]

By mid-July the LCPs were suffering from their prolonged, heavy use and the crews were exhausted, even though they had taken it in turns to work alternate nights. The craft were withdrawn for a refit at Poole and the sailors given leave. Colin fondly remembered the flotilla's crews who were mainly 'young – in their twenties – and wartime sailors only. Yet their dogged good humour and ability to make the best of unpleasant circumstances were marvellous to behold.'[21]

One of the warships that Colin gave smoke cover to during the summer of 1944 was the cruiser HMS *Belfast* (now a floating museum in London). It was an:

exquisite pleasure, for a junior RNVR officer, of being piped over the side as a commanding officer. I was then ushered into conference with Admiral Sir Frederick Dalrymple-Hamilton [Commander 10th Cruiser Squadron and Second-in-Command Home Fleet] and Captain Parham [skipper of HMS *Belfast*] and asked to outline my smoke-screen intentions for the night and for the proposed bombardment of Le Havre the next day.'[22]

As the campaign progressed Colin was to become even more intimately involved with Le Havre. By August the flotilla were sailing off Normandy again but because Allied forces had advanced sufficiently far inland the enemy's air threat had considerably diminished. Consequently, there was less need for smoke protection and in September the flotilla was, much to their surprise, given the task of minesweeping the harbour at Le Havre (Operation Broom). It was considered that the comparatively small size of the LCP (L) (approximately 37ft x 11ft x 3ft) made it highly suited to this specialist task within the confines of the harbour. The flotilla were given a few days to prepare for their new role and on 14 September 1944 six of its boats 'were the first Allied vessels to enter Le Havre since June 1940'.[23]

They expected to find what were termed Katie mines, as these had previously been encountered at Cherbourg. These were difficult to deal with, 'a spongy type of rope coloured pale green ran up from the mine and floated on the surface. Very difficult to see against the colour of the sea.'[24] The idea being that the rope would become entangled with ships entering the harbour and once sufficient pressure was exerted the mine would explode.

In the event the operation proved an anti-climax as a thorough sweep revealed no mines. During it Colin had assumed temporary command of the flotilla as the CO was on compassionate leave:

A very interesting experience for somebody only twenty-three, coming up twenty-four. Twelve boats, sixty-six men, and I look back on that and think 'How the hell did I cope with that', and its ludicrous really. A young man of so little experience, and yet naval training and traditions and attitudes . . . you know what to do . . .[25]

After their deployment at Le Havre the flotilla went back to HMS *Tormentor* and by 1945 were on the point of being disbanded. However, in February of that year the services of their small craft were once more in demand. The unit found itself re-designated 821 LCVP (Landing Craft Vehicle/Personnel) Fotilla and was sent to Antwerp. From there their main task was to assist the Army in transporting Bailey bridge sections along canals and rivers, particularly the Rhine and later the Elbe. The Bailey bridge was a standard piece of bridging equipment employed by sappers and several sections together with pontoons could form a crossing on even the broadest of rivers.[26]

After VE-Day the flotilla was disbanded and several of its personnel posted to the Far East. For Colin his war service, particularly aboard an LCP, had been a formative experience. As an officer in a flotilla equipped with such small craft he had to endure the same level of discomfort and danger as his men. There was simply no scope for having a separate cabin or wardroom and he ate the same food. Likewise, 'If you were on a big exercise or an operation and you were going to have a break, you just had to squat down in the cockpit where the driving seat was as they did.'[27]

After the war Colin and his wife, whom he had married in 1943, settled in south London where he worked as Assistant Secretary at Middlesex Hospital. Subsequently, he became an executive in the Pirelli Tyre Company, a post where his Oxford education and wartime naval experience were of value. In 1972 they moved from London to Repton when the company re-located.

Colin and his wife were founder members of the Repton Village History Group, an interest that dominated their lives. He developed a particular fascination with Caulke Abbey, editing the journals of Sir George Crewe, published in 1995 as *The Squire of Caulke Abbey* (Scarthin Books). Additionally, Colin was member of his local church and was pleased to be able to show off its architecture when the opportunity arose.

As Repton made ready to celebrate the millennium, he was instrumental in plans to commission a war memorial to commemorate the forty-nine villagers lost serving their country during the world wars. Before his death in 2008 he had experienced the added personal satisfaction of being involved in at least one large-scale reunion of his former wartime flotilla at HMS *Tormentor*.[28]

Researching Colin Kitching

As with any wartime serviceman or woman, there are various documents relevant to Colin's naval service at TNA. These largely deal with operational and administrative matters. For example, ADM 1/10709 contains brief correspondence dealing with the establishment of HMS *Tormentor*. Within ADM 1 Admiralty, MOD, Navy Department, Correspondence and Papers can also be found material on HMS *Edinburgh*, particularly relating to its sinking. While ADM 179 Admiralty: Portsmouth Station: Correspondence contains documentation on Operation Starkey. Similarly, records on Operations Jubilee (Dieppe) and Neptune (the naval component of D-Day) can be found within ADM 199 Admiralty: War History Cases and Papers, Second World War.

In July 2002 Colin was interviewed on behalf of SWWEC by Dr Peter Liddle and a copy of the transcript is available at their archives. Additionally, he deposited a series of typed recollections on various aspects of his naval service that provide an insight into his personal war experience. A further source for this type of information is via the BBC website. Since the sixtieth anniversary of the end of the Second World War the BBC have sought to collate a record of ordinary people's reminiscences at: www.bbc.co.uk/ww2.

Another extremely useful and reliable website can be found at: www.naval-history.net which incorporates features such as service histories of individual warships. Likewise, H. T. Lenton and J. J. Colledge's *Warships of World War II* (Ian Allan Ltd, 1980) provides much useful information, including details on landing craft such as the LCP (L). Admiral Sir Reginald H. S. Bacon (ed.), *Britain's Glorious Navy* (Odhams Press Ltd, *c*. 1940–5) incorporates several interesting chapters, including one on 'Mines and Mine Sweeping'. Eric J. Grove's 'A Service Vindicated, 1939–1946' in *The Oxford History Illustrated History of the Royal Navy* (Oxford University Press, 1995) is a wide-ranging chapter on the Second World War, useful as historical background when researching anyone who served in the wartime Navy.

Ronald Lewin's *Ultra Goes to War: The Secret Story* (Book Club Associates, 1978) and Charles Cruickshank's *Deception in World War Two* (Book Club Associates, 1979) are two eminently accessible accounts dealing with aspects of intelligence and deception, including Operation Starkey and the seizing of the Enigma code tables from the *Munchen*.

Of interest are two articles: R. W. Thompson's 'Massacre at Dieppe' and Lieutenant Colonel Herbert Fairlie Wood's 'The Canadians at Dieppe' in *Purnell's History of the Second World War* (Phoebus Publishing Ltd, 1967), Vol. 3, No. 8 which provide an introduction to this tragic raid. So does Tim Saunders's *Dieppe Operation Jubilee – Channel Ports* (Pen & Sword, 2005), which acts as both a guide book and a stimulus for further reading on the subject. Similarly, Cornelius Ryan's *The Longest Day* (Wordsworth Editions, 1999), first published in 1959, provides the classic narrative of D-Day, including reference to the assistance given by naval forces.

Notes

1. Second World War Experience Centre, Acc. No. LEEWW 2003-2250, transcript of tape 1537, interview with Colin Kitching by Dr Peter Liddle, July 2002, p. 4.
2. For further details on HMS *Edinburgh* see H. T. Lenton and J. J. Colledge, *Warships of World War II* (Ian Allan Ltd, 1980), pp. 23–5, 49, and www.naval-history.net/xGM-chrono-06CL-Edinburgh.htm.
3. SWWEC, Acc. No. LEEWW 2003-2250, transcript of tape 1537, interview with Colin Kitching by Dr Peter Liddle, July 2002, p. 5.
4. Ibid., p. 8.
5. Ibid.
6. SWWEC, Acc. No. LEEWW 2003-2250, 'Enigmatic Anniversary' recollections compiled by Colin Kitching, January 2001, p. 2.
7. SWWEC, Acc. No. LEEWW 2003-2250, transcript of tape 1537, interview with Colin Kitching by Dr Peter Liddle, July 2002, p. 11.
8. Lenton and Colledge, *Warships of World War II*, p. 619.
9. R. W. Thompson, 'Massacre at Dieppe' in *Purnell's History of the Second World War* (Phoebus Publishing Ltd, 1967), Vol. 3, No. 8, p. 1101.
10. SWWEC, Acc. No. LEEWW 2003-2250, transcript of tape 1537, interview with Colin Kitching by Dr Peter Liddle, July 2002, pp. 13–14.
11. Ibid., p. 14.
12. Ibid.
13. SWWEC, Acc. No. LEEWW 2003-2250, 'Excursion to Dieppe, 1942', recollections compiled by Colin Kitching, n.d., pp. 3–4.
14. Ibid., p. 5.
15. SWWEC, Acc. No. LEEWW 2003-2250, transcript of tape 1537, interview with Colin Kitching by Dr Peter Liddle, July 2002, p. 15.
16. For details of Operation Starkey (9 September 1943) see Charles Cruickshank's *Deception in World War Two* (Book Club Associates, 1979), pp. 62–74.
17. SWWEC, Acc. No. LEEWW 2003-2250, transcript of tape 1538, interview with Colin Kitching by Dr Peter Liddle, July 2002, p. 1.
18. SWWEC, Acc. No. LEEWW 2003-2250, 'D-Day 1944: A Personal Memoir', recollections compiled by Colin Kitching, May 1994, p. 1.
19. Ibid.
20. SWWEC, Acc. No. LEEWW 2003-2250, transcript of tape 1538, interview with Colin Kitching by Dr Peter Liddle, July 2002, p. 3.
21. SWWEC, Acc. No. LEEWW 2003-2250, 'D-Day 1944: A Personal Memoir', recollections compiled by Colin Kitching, May 1994, p. 2.
22. Ibid., p. 3.

23. SWWEC, Acc. No. LEEWW 2003-2250, 'Versatile LCPs', recollections compiled by Colin Kitching, May 2002, p. 2.
24. SWWEC, Acc. No. LEEWW 2003-2250, transcript of tape 1538, interview with Colin Kitching by Dr Peter Liddle, July 2002, p. 3.
25. Ibid., p. 4.
26. For further details of the Bailey bridge, see Lieutenant Colonel George Forty's *British Army Handbook 1939–1945* (Sutton Publishing, 2002), pp. 282–6.
27. SWWEC, Acc. No. LEEWW 2003-2250, transcript of tape 1538, interview with Colin Kitching by Dr Peter Liddle, July 2002, p. 5.
28. Obituaries and tributes for Colin Kitching can be found at: www.thisisannouncements.co.uk and www.reptonvillage.org.uk.

Chapter 13

A Medical Officer on D-Day –
Dr Ian D. Campbell

D uring the Second World War most fighting was experienced 'by a remarkably small proportion of troops whose casualties were very high'.[1] Partly this was because far more men were employed in logistical tasks than directly involved in combat. A 'British infantry division contained 17,000 men but only 4,000 of these, less than a quarter, actually carried a rifle and bayonet'.[2] However, even support troops could become non-battle casualties through accidents or disease.

By 1944 British Army medical services were able to draw upon extensive experience from other theatres, notably the Mediterranean and Western Desert. Field ambulance units had improved mobility and the RAMC was better equipped to conduct surgery in forward areas. This saved time and increased the chances of casualties recovering successfully. By the 1940s, for example, 'abdominal wounds, which half a century ago were usually fatal and brought death three times out of four in World War I, were healed in over 50 per cent of cases'.[3]

Similarly, as the war progressed doctors could rely on a range of sulphonamides (sulphur-based drugs) and penicillin to treat disease and infections. These had been absent in previous conflicts. Inoculations were given against serious conditions such as typhus, smallpox and tetanus. While VD, that traditional hindrance to any army's effectiveness, was eventually treated with penicillin so that 'the wastage in men was greatly reduced'.[4]

The introduction of blood transfusion services and new techniques in the use of plaster had further positive implications for the wounded. The Army also employed psychiatrists 'to deal not only with battle casualties . . . but to assist in the rehabilitation of the limbless'.[5] Yet despite these advances the challenges facing military doctors was still immense, particularly as treatment, including surgery, frequently had to be conducted near the front line.

Matters were further complicated because a soldier with a 'slight' wound was at risk of it becoming 'severe' if he was not promptly treated and if necessary evacuated. Typically, the severity of wounds varied depending on the weapon used and the part of the body hit:

> grenades cause a lower ratio of 'severe' wounds than bullets (rifle or machine gun) while shells and trench mortars cause the highest ratio of 'severe' wounds. Wounds of chest and abdomen are more likely to be 'severe' than 'slight', while the reverse is the case as regards wounds of hands, feet, face, etc.[6]

Ian D. Campbell was born during 1916 in Duirinish near the Kyle of Lochalsh, Ross and Cromarty. His family moved to Buealy, near Inverness when he was 12 when his father obtained a new position as a bank agent. Subsequently, he was educated at Dingwall Academy and the University of Edinburgh.

Initially, he studied BSc level chemistry, physics and biology at university before switching to medicine. He enjoyed the change as it gave him an exemption from the above subjects. Instead, he concentrated on anatomy and botany with the latter entailing regular classes at Edinburgh Botanic Gardens.

While a student he became aware of the rising political tensions in Europe, particularly the Spanish Civil War, 'a number of my colleagues and friends were disappearing for three or six months at a time. Some dressed in fascist uniform and some with lovely red ties [communists], . . . were there before the war started'.[7]

Life was good with plenty of sporting and social activities to enjoy. He qualified as a doctor in July 1939 then acquired a job as a locum general practitioner in Cromarty on the Black Isle. The presiding doctor, a friend of his father's, had become ill and desperately asked for assistance. In summer the practice was not busy which allowed him to play golf and tennis regularly.

This idyllic lifestyle was ruptured by the outbreak of war. His ambition of following a peacetime medical career that would ultimately see him ending up a Highland GP had to be shelved. Instead, he took an interim job as a house surgeon at St Luke's Hospital, Bradford and expected to be called up swiftly.

However, there was little immediate effort to employ doctors for the armed forces. He worked at St Luke's for sixteen months before joining the Army at Beckett's Park, Leeds in January 1941. There he spent two weeks learning drill and basic military discipline. The doctors drew playing cards to see who would receive the postings on offer.

Ian volunteered for the Middle East but was unsuccessful. He ended up in Londonderry, Northern Ireland with a field ambulance attached to 53rd Wessex Division. The port was busy at the 'start of the Battle of the Atlantic and there was a destroyer flotilla and corvettes and plenty of other ships . . . they used to go out for 14 days and come back and refit for two days . . . and we got to know the Medical Officers on these ships and it was a bustling place'.[8] Training had an accent on physical fitness with long route marches. Additionally, Ian's 'CO was a great enthusiast for getting everyone to go cross country motorcycling and that . . . sort of thing'.[9]

From Londonderry he was posted to Oulleston Park, Northampton, a former leisure park. This was a good billet with a swimming pool and dance hall. While there he received further training and was involved in large-scale exercises between Southern and Eastern Command. The emphasis was on mobility, speed and treating casualties effectively and preparing them for evacuation.

Additionally, Ian experienced 'special training'. This included assault courses under realistic battlefield conditions with an acceptance that there would be casualties:

The Austin K 2/Y heavy ambulance 4 x 2 was affectionately known as the 'Katie' and could accommodate four stretcher cases, eight sitting cases or a combination of both plus medical staff. (Author's photograph)

One in Penistone in the December of 1941 which was a pretty tough one in the winter. I mean it was run by the KRRCs [King's Royal Rifle Corps] and they really got us to understand what fire under rifle ammunition was like [Battle Inoculation] and it was pretty hectic, and I was supposed to have done quite well in that and I got onto other ones.[10]

By 1941 the 'British Army at home was full of young men [like Ian Campbell] who knew that they faced a difficult and dangerous task in defeating the German Army and feared they were not being properly prepared for it.'[11] Realistic, tough training such as this, and that conducted at 'Battle Schools' around the country, went some way towards dispelling such concerns.

Subsequently, Ian was posted to East Grinstead, Sussex and attached to 6th Armoured Division then being readied for deployment to the Middle East. However, this posting was short-lived and he soon ended up in Paisley. Here he joined Number 2 Field Dressing Station (No. 2 FDS), tasked with dealing with casualties requiring treatment in a battle area prior to their evacuation.

His FDS was part of Number 7 Beach Landing Group (No. 7 BLG) destined to be deployed during the Normandy Landings. The BLG was responsible for organising and administering facilities on the beach-head so that assault troops could advance freely. Typically, this entailed tasks such as mine clearance; marking roads and exits; recovering vehicles; and assisting with the landing of follow-up troops and stores. Specialists including engineers, signals and medical personnel were attached to every BLG.

During 1943–4 No. 7 BLG was involved in intensive training for their role in Operation Overlord, the Allied invasion of Normandy. Latterly, much of it was done in conjunction with the assault troops to be landed on D-Day. 'Wet and dry-shod landing exercises were undertaken on a variety of beaches including Studland Bay, Bracklesham Bay and Slapton Sands in the south of England and in Scotland, in Irvine Bay . . .'.[12] Often training entailed the unit being split up with personnel being allocated to different ships for their 'crossing'. This was advantageous as medical personnel became familiar with many of the units they would be supporting on D-Day. Ian particularly remembered a difficult exercise at Studland Bay:

we went from Southampton, and usually in the winter it was very stormy round about the Needles . . . and we got over to Studland Bay and the Infantry went in . . . They had a sort of simulated exercise. They had focal points to take . . . We for our part, having landed usually you went up over your shoulders because there were ruddles [hidden deep pools] on the beach. I had to deal with fake casualties. There were a lot of fake casualties which we tried to simulate treatment and evacuate to hospital which was supposed to be a military hospital somewhere.[13]

In October 1943 No. 2 FDS were allotted a wood near Winchester and stayed there except when on exercises. Then in May 1944 new vehicles were received, waterproofed and loaded. Personnel were issued large rucksacks for supplies, medical equipment and their personal kit. These weighed approximately 100lb which ensured men needed to be physically fit to carry them in action, especially when landing in deep water off a beach. Additionally, the 'considerable quantities of condoms . . . issued to medical units, and not required for immediate use . . . provided an excellent method of waterproofing small items of equipment, such as syringes and watches'.[14]

While awaiting embarkation for D-Day several members of No. 2 FDS were surprised when:

after our final briefing and the unit transport had left for Southampton docks, some of us were sunbathing in a gap in our wood when a small group of people came through the trees, including a stout chap wearing a familiar hat. One of our officers, in a state of almost total undress, grabbed a hat, sprang to attention and saluted exclaiming 'Christ its Churchill'.[15]

The Prime Minister chatted to them, shared a drink in the NAAFI, but seemed to be in a bleak mood. Later, he appeared at Southampton docks and hailed Ian and the other troops wishing them 'Good luck' while throwing up his famous 'V' sign.

On 5 June 1944 the landings were postponed for 24 hours owing to bad weather. Many troops including Ian were left temporarily 'stranded' aboard their ships. Hyoscine, a drug administered by the British to thwart 'motion sickness', was unfortunately ineffective during this 'prolonged ordeal'.[16]

Ian was struck by the sheer number and variety of craft involved. He was aboard a former cross-Channel steamer that was sailing next to a French destroyer blasting out *The Marseillaise*. On D-Day he was to transfer to a LCT to transport him to the beach-head. He was further moved by how on the eve of battle religion suddenly came to the fore. Many troops, some of whom had previously been disinterested or even hostile towards it, discovered that church services and prayers assumed a heightened sense of importance when faced with the imminent possibility that they might not survive action in Normandy.

Commandos from 1st Special Service Brigade wade ashore from their landing craft on D-Day. (Taylor Library)

In the early hours of 6 June 1944 (D-Day) Ian waited in his ship about 6 miles off Juno Beach. It was imperative that the medical component of the landings worked effectively or else disaster might have ensued if casualties were not treated and successfully evacuated. The complexities of the medical operation alone can be gauged by the fact that one British assault division landed '1,154 members of the RAMC in the first wave'.[17]

At 10am Ian landed on Juno Beach in the wake of 1st Battalion the Canadian Scottish Regiment from 3rd Canadian Division. 'Initially the scene seemed similar to that on an exercise but it soon became apparent the wounded and dead were not *fake casualties* and the destruction of landing craft along the beach was devastating.'[18] Ian made contact with a Beach Dressing Station that had landed previously and proceeded to the village of Graye-sur-Mer where he was to establish No. 2 FDS with the intention of facilitating the evacuation of casualties.

However, this had to be delayed as the beach was under small arms fire, particularly from enemy snipers, and many of the engineers who were clearing it became casualties. Ian spent the morning assisting the medical staff at the Beach Dressing Station. At about midday he received permission from the BLG commander to advance towards the village hall at Graye-sur-Mer that was to be used as a FDS. He relied on the detailed maps he had been issued with which featured fictitious names (for security) and identified beach exits and local landmarks.

En route he and his sergeant were surprised to encounter a small figure heading towards them. It was the village priest. Recognising their Red Cross arm bands, he explained that, 'the Germans were there and they left about six o clock and we had been through the village hall and they had cleared it for booby traps . . . we are just scrubbing it out just now, and it will be ready for you any moment now'.[19] Sister Madeline, a French nurse who had been away from Caen visiting friends, also reported for duty at the village hall.

Both of these events were a massive help. By early afternoon the FDS was operational, 'casualties came streaming in. A lot of them were absolutely exhausted, but there were some who were very, very seriously injured.'[20] In the evening a Field Surgical Unit that performed life-saving operations was established in an adjacent barn and supported by a Blood Transfusion Unit.

The FDS's primary function was 'to get essential surgery done. Treatment done, and to evacuate to UK as quickly as possible, and this was done through the navy.'[21] Initially, hospital ships could not be docked as space was unavailable and evacuation by air proved impractical. Consequently, LSTs were run onto the beach and as soon as the vehicles had been unloaded they took on board casualties. Folding racks could accommodate 350 lying cases and blood plasma and medical equipment were stored in the stern ready for use on the return voyage. The casualties could be brought onto LSTs via DUKWs (amphibious trucks) and transported to hospitals in Britain as speedily as possible.

On D-Day alone 855 casualties were evacuated via this system. By the end of June this extemporised form of casualty evacuation was no longer necessary. The number of medical units in Normandy had grown and it proved possible to use general hospitals in theatre. With the expansion of the beach-head, casualties could also start to be evacuated by air using Dakota aircraft.

Ian recalled that his first priority was to 'build up to a unit that we could take about 600 with tents [i.e. 600 patients]'.[22] In this they were aided as the village hall was surrounded by an orchard. However, during 18–21 June a heavy storm in the Channel destroyed the Mulberry harbour at St-Laurent which severely hampered the Allies's supply system, including the evacuation of casualties. Graye-sur-Mer was full of wounded in great discomfort and desperate to get away from the battle area. For the next few weeks No. 2 FDS performed its 'main role as a CEP (Casualty Evacuation Point) receiving, reviewing, treating where necessary and evacuating casualties'.[23]

Although consumed by his work in treating the casualties, Ian was moved by the human cost of the campaign, particularly the role of the padres in dealing with the dead. Some of the Canadian officers who became casualties on D-Day were known to him from pre-invasion exercises. Additionally, one casualty blown up on landing by a mine took time to identify and turned out to be an Edinburgh medical graduate he had known well.

Subsequently, No. 2 FDS was transferred to the Chateaux de Vaux, a former children's sanatorium, close to the beach which provided more suitable accommodation and space for additional tents to cope with large numbers of wounded. It was to act as the single Casualty Evacuation Point for the British and Canadian fronts. Until the military general hospitals could function at Bayeaux, invaluable work was conducted by the medical units based at the chateaux under the umbrella organisation of No. 2 FDS.

As Ian noted, a routine was adopted, 'where we received and assessed casualties, . . . and fed them, and if they were fit to move they were cared for until an LST arrived and beached, and we loaded them on'.[24] Treatment in many cases included the administering of the new 'magic drug' penicillin, supplies of which had been especially reserved for Normandy casualties.

Despite having to face up to the human horrors of the campaign there was a light-hearted side to serving in a forward medical unit. American naval crews operating at Juno Beach regularly sought 'German trophies' such as helmets or *Achtung Minen* signs. A barter system emerged. For example, a German helmet, of which there were plentiful supplies from enemy wounded, could be worth a large amount of beef. Soon the FDS was well known for the quality of its food. However, when the supply of genuine *Achtung Minen* signs, with their distinctive skull and crossbones emblem, ran out it was necessary to detail the unit carpenter to 'manufacture' several more from leftover wooden boxes.

Ian remained at the chateaux for the remainder of the Normandy Campaign and when Paris fell on 25 August it appeared that the FDS was to stay there. However, a few weeks later, 'we got a message to move from the beach and we moved straight through France in a day and a half and got to Amiens, where we spent our second night, and then we went onto Brussels'.[25]

They arrived there shortly after that city had been liberated and there were crowds of joyful civilians lining the streets as the FDS convoy passed headed for Louvain. En route a dispatch rider stopped them and instructed them 'to return to the airport'. It was 17 September 1944 and Operation Market Garden had been launched. Allied airborne forces were attempting to seize key bridges over the Rhine and so enable a rapid advance by land forces into Germany on a narrow front. From No. 2 FDS's perspective this necessitated establishing the same organisation as had existed in Normandy, only this time all casualties would be evacuated by air not sea.

Ian and his unit remained in Belgium during the winter of 1944–5 and helped treat casualties. This included those arising from the 'Battle of the Bulge', Hitler's last-ditch offensive in the Ardennes designed to seize Antwerp and thwart Allied progress in northern Europe. As the war progressed No. 2 FDS followed the Allied advance into Germany conducting their invaluable treatment and evacuation work. South of Bremen the unit encountered casualties from the concentration camp at Belsen, including American troops taken prisoner when reconnoitring across the Rhine earlier that winter. These men were 'really absolutely skin and bone and in a very bad way, and we had to try and get fluid, limited fluid, into them so that they could survive'.[26]

One of Ian's other duties included the supervision of a 600-bed hospital in Delmenhorst, Germany that was full of enemy wounded. He was fascinated 'to see how they classified their wounded . . . They were all classified according to the operation undertaken and not according to their state of illness [or wound]. It didn't matter as long as they got them all neatly classified . . . it was being run very well.'[27]

During the campaign in North-West Europe the 'recovery rate for all wounded [in the British Army] was . . . 94 per cent'.[28] Partly this was a consequence of the planning processes that went into operations. However, it was also due to the efforts of doctors like Ian, plus other RAMC staff at field hospitals, and all those troops involved in the evacuation of casualties.

After the war Ian continued to serve in the Army as a senior Medical Officer and saw active service in Palestine. By 1948 he was demobbed and eventually appointed to the Leeds Regional Hospital Board with an office in The Headrow, and later at the former Queen's Hotel, Harrogate. He enjoyed his work with its regional responsibilities and was involved in the planning of a new hospital in Huddersfield at an exciting time when the NHS was in its infancy.

In 1993 he re-visited the Normandy beaches and was pleased to meet the Mayor of Graye-sur-Mer, who as an 11-year-old boy had helped move stores and stretchers at No. 2 FDS. He was delighted to discover that Sister Madeline, the French nurse who had assisted them, was the Mayor's godmother and King George VI had awarded her the MBE for her work. The priest who had offered them the village hall was still alive too, although he had taken on another parish.

Reflecting on his wartime experiences Ian noted that the Army helped him to deal with the administrative aspects of his post-war medical career. Additionally, as a young man it gave him confidence and was an education. While a RAMC officer he came to know about the troops and their families, particularly when censoring letters. As he put it, 'you had to glimpse through the various letters written by the troops and you saw really, you learnt a lot about life'.[29]

Researching Dr Ian D. Campbell

John Ellis's *The Sharp End: The Fighting Man in World War II* (Pimlico, 1990) contains an absorbing chapter on casualties with particular reference to the experience of British and American soldiers. By contrast, Anthony Cotterell's *R.A.M.C.* (Hutchinson & Co. (Publishers) Ltd, n.d. *c.* late 1943) was intended for popular consumption during the war. While pre-dating D-Day, it does outline the British approach to dealing with casualties and explains some of the medical advances made during the war. It includes detail on the personal experiences of RAMC personnel, especially from the French Campaign, 1940 and Western Desert, 1940–2.

Peter Lovegrove's *Not Least in the Crusade: A Short History of the RAMC* (Gale & Polden Ltd, 1954) outlines the role played by the Army's medical services during 1939–45 and includes a section on Normandy. Gale & Polden Ltd specialised in producing regimental histories and books of a semi-official nature on military topics. Redmond McLaughlin's *The Royal Army Medical Corps* (Leo Cooper, 1972) is a general history of the RAMC, that forms part of the 'Famous Regiments Series' published by Leo Cooper, and includes chapters on the Second World War.

R. H. Ahrenfeldt's *Psychiatry in the British Army in the Second World War* (Routledge & Kegan Paul, 1958) is a medical history on the application of psychiatry to the wartime military, including the treatment of battle exhaustion or shell shock. Similarly, Timothy Harrison Place's *Military Training in the British Army, 1940–1944: From Dunkirk to D-Day* (Frank Cass, 2000) is a comprehensive analysis of the state of training in the wartime Army in Britain. It discusses the role of the battle schools that provided realistic, tough training akin to that experienced by Ian during 1941–4. All of the above should be available at the IWM (Department of Books). Alternatively, you might like to try second-hand bookshops, search on the Internet or use an inter library loan.

An outline of Dr Ian Campbell's experiences was gleaned from his interview with Dr Peter Liddle conducted on behalf of SWWEC in April 2002. A transcript of this is available at their archives, together with Campbell's article 'The Evacuation of Casualties from a Normandy Beach June–August 1944' in *D-Day Recollections Reproduced in the Proceedings of the Royal College of Physicians of Edinburgh*, Vol. 24 (1994), which neatly complements the interview material.

Information on the RAMC can be found at TNA, particularly in WO 177 Medical Services. This contains historical records, including the War Diary for No. 2 FDS spanning March 1943–February 1946, which documents the movements and work of that unit. In WO 32 General Series are numerous other files on medical services that largely relate to administrative issues.

Anyone interested in wartime medical services might wish to visit the Wellcome Library, London which houses a rich archive on medical history, including papers relating to the RAMC. For more information see their website at: www.library.wellcome.ac.uk. Likewise, the Army Medical Services Museum at Keogh Barracks in Surrey holds records on RAMC units but not those detailing the service of individuals. Should you wish to visit them, please find further details at: www.ams-museum.org.uk.

Finally, the following publications provide useful background on D-Day and the Normandy Campaign, particularly for anybody who wishes to research an individual involved in that theatre of operations or visit the battlefields: Brigadier Peter Young, *D-Day* (Bison Books Ltd, 1985); Tonie and Valmai Holt, *The Visitor's Guide to Normandy Landing Beaches* (Moorland Publishing Co. Ltd, 1990); John Man, *The Penguin Atlas of D-Day and the Normandy Campaign* (Penguin Books, 1994); and Anthony Beevor, *D-Day: The Battle For Normandy* (Penguin Viking, 2009).

Notes

1. John Ellis, *The Sharp End: The Fighting Man in World War II* (Pimlico, 1990), p. 162.
2. Ibid., p. 157.
3. Peter Lovegrove, *Not Least in the Crusade: A Short History of the RAMC* (Gale & Polden Ltd, 1954), p. 56.
4. Redmond McLaughlin, *The Royal Army Medical Corps* (Leo Cooper, 1972), p. 80.
5. Lovegrove, *Not Least in the Crusade*, p. 77.
6. Anthony Cotterell, *R.A.M.C.* (Hutchinson & Co. (Publishers) Ltd, n.d. *c.* late 1943), p. 15.

7. Second World War Experience Centre, Acc. No. 2000-447, transcript of taped interview, tape 1383 with Dr I. D. Campbell by Dr Peter Liddle, April 2002, p. 2.

8. Ibid., p. 4.

9. Ibid.

10. Ibid., p. 5.

11. Timothy Harrison Place, *Military Training in the British Army, 1940–1944: From Dunkirk to D-Day* (Frank Cass, 2000), p. 61.

12. Dr Ian D. Campbell, 'The Evacuation of Casualties from a Normandy Beach June–August 1944' in *D-Day Recollections Reproduced in the Proceedings of the Royal College of Physicians of Edinburgh*, Vol. 24 (1994), p. 1.

13. SWWEC, Acc. No. 2000-447, transcript of taped interview, tape 1383 with Dr I. D. Campbell by Dr Peter Liddle, April 2002, p. 6.

14. Campbell, 'The Evacuation of Casualties from a Normandy Beach June–August 1944', p. 1.

15. Ibid., p. 2.

16. McLaughlin, *The Royal Army Medical Corps*, pp. 87–8.

17. Ibid., p. 89.

18. Campbell, 'The Evacuation of Casualties from a Normandy Beach June– August 1944', p. 2.

19. SWWEC, Acc. No. 2000-447, transcript of taped interview, tape 1383 with Dr I. D. Campbell by Dr Peter Liddle, April 2002, p. 8.

20. Ibid.

21. Ibid., p. 9.

22. Ibid.

23. Campbell, 'The Evacuation of Casualties from a Normandy Beach June– August 1944', p. 3.

24. SWWEC, Acc. No. 2000-447, transcript of taped interview, tape 1383 with Dr I. D. Campbell by Dr Peter Liddle, April 2002, p. 9.

25. Ibid., p. 10.

26. Ibid., p. 11.

27. Ibid.

28. Lovegrove, *Not Least in the Crusade*, p. 72.

29. SWWEC Acc. No. 2000-447, Transcript of Interview with Campbell, p. 12.

FURTHER READING

Aldrich, Richard J., *Witness to War: Diaries of the Second World War in Europe and the Middle East*, Doubleday, 2004

Armitage, Michael, *The Royal Air Force: An illustrated History*, Brockhampton Press, 1996

Chandler, David and Beckett, Ian (eds), *The Oxford Illustrated History of the British Army*, Oxford University Press, 1994

Chant, Christopher, *The Encyclopedia of Code Names of World War Two*, Routledge & Keegan Paul, 1986

Fowler, Simon, *Tracing Your Army Ancestors*, Pen & Sword, 2006

Fussel, Paul, *Wartime: Understanding and Behaviour in the Second World War*, Oxford University Press, 1989

Hallows, Ian S., *Regiments and Corps of the British Army*, New Orchard, 1994

Hill, J. R. (ed.), *The Oxford Illustrated History of the Royal Navy*, Oxford University Press, 1995

Holland, James, *Heroes: The Greatest Generation and the Second World War*, Harper Perennial, 2007

Keegan, John, *The Second World War*, Pimlico, 1997

Pappalardo, Bruno, *Tracing Your Naval Ancestors*, Public Record Office (TNA), 2003

Parkinson, Roger, *Encyclopaedia of Modern War*, Paladin, 1979

Spencer, William, *Air Force Records: A Guide for Family Historians*, TNA, 2008

—, *Army Records: A Guide for Family Historians*, TNA, 2008

—, *Medals: The Researcher's Guide*, TNA, 2008

Tomaselli, Phil, *Tracing Your Air Force Ancestors*, Pen & Sword, 2007

Weinberg, Gerhard L., *A World At Arms: A Global History of World War II*, Cambridge University Press, 1995

INDEX